Interpreting Indicators of Rangeland Health

Version 4

By

Mike Pellant
Rangeland Ecologist
Bureau of Land Management
Boise, Idaho

David A. Pyke
Research Ecologist
U.S. Geological Survey
Forest and Rangeland Ecosystem
  Science Center
Corvallis, Oregon

Patrick Shaver
Rangeland Management Specialist
Natural Resources Conservation Service
Portland, Oregon

Jeffrey E. Herrick
Research Scientist
Agricultural Research Service
Jornada Experimental Range
Las Cruces, New Mexico

Produced By

United States Department of the Interior
Bureau of Land Management
National Science and Technology Center
Division of Science Integration
Branch of Publishing Services
P. O. Box 25047
Denver, Colorado

Technical Reference 1734-6
2005

Suggested citation:

Pellant, M., P. Shaver, D.A. Pyke, and J.E. Herrick. 2005. Interpreting indicators of rangeland health, version 4. Technical Reference 1734-6. U.S. Department of the Interior, Bureau of Land Management, National Science and Technology Center, Denver, CO. BLM/WO/ST-00/001+1734/REV05. 122 pp.

Acknowledgments

Interagency coordination between the Bureau of Land Management (BLM), the Natural Resources Conservation Service (NRCS), the Agricultural Research Service (ARS), and the USGS Forest and Rangeland Ecosystem Science Center was essential to successfully completing this document. The order of authors cited for this publication is a reflection of the amount of time spent on document organization and preparation for Version 4.0, not the important and equal contribution that each author made to the scientific and procedural content of this technical reference.

The authors want to again acknowledge and thank all of the previous contributors to Version 3 and earlier versions of *Interpreting Indicators of Rangeland Health* for their valuable input, which has cumulatively added to the quality and usefulness of this technical reference. As the concept of rangeland health continues to evolve and mature, the application of this concept and protocol will also evolve and be reflected in future versions of the document.

The changes in Version 4 reflect input from several hundred workshop participants in the United States, Canada, and Mexico, as well as numerous individual discussions and evaluations and scientific review through the USGS peer-review process. The document also benefited from significant input from the National Science Foundation-funded Jornada Basin Long-Term Ecological Research Project. The BLM's National Training Center, under the leadership of Julie Decker, provided support for numerous interagency training sessions that provided the authors with the feedback used to move from Version 3 to Version 4. Individuals who reviewed or contributed to significant modifications of Version 4 include Jack Alexander, Brandon Bestelmeyer, Peter Dunwiddie, Kirk Gadzia, Sherm Karl, Patrick McCarthy, Mark Miller, Laura Burkett, Peter Russell, George Ruyle, Pete Sundt, Arlene Tugel, and Bob Unnasch. Cynthia Dalzell reviewed and edited several drafts of this document and is recognized for her contribution.

Thanks to Kathy Rohling and Janine Koselak of BLM's National Science and Technology Center for the editing, design, and layout of this technical reference and to BLM's National Business Center for managing the production aspects of the final document.

Preface

Version 4 of Interpreting Indicators of Rangeland Health, Technical Reference 1734-6, is the second published edition of this technique. It follows the recommendations published in Pyke et al. (2002). The indicators are unchanged from Version 3, allowing this document to replace Version 3 even in areas where the evaluation process has already begun.

The changes in Version 4 are designed to improve the consistency in the application of the process. The most significant modification is the replacement of the Ecological Reference Area Worksheet with the Reference Sheet (Appendix 2). The Reference Sheet facilitates consistent application of the process on each ecological site by integrating all available sources of data and knowledge to generate a single range of reference conditions for each indicator.

We have removed the Species Dominance Worksheet (Version 3, Appendix 4), since the information gained from this worksheet is similar to the information in the Functional/Structural Groups Sheet. We have included cells for noxious weeds and invasive plants in the Functional/Structural Groups Sheet (Version 4, Appendix 3). This allows users to continue to document the presence and abundance of invasive species for their records.

The Cover Sheet (Version 3, Appendix 3) has been deleted and information on collecting quantitative data is deferred to other publications.

Based on a more thorough review of the literature, we have switched the attribute assignment for the litter movement indicator from Hydrologic Function to Soil/Site Stability in Version 4, Appendix 1.

In Version 3, Appendix 1, all of the indicator rating categories except "Extreme departure from the Ecological Site Description/Reference Area" implied that the category included a range of values. This implication came either from the title (for example None to Slight departure) or from the position within the range of the other categories (for example Moderate was between Slight to Moderate and Moderate to Extreme), but the fifth category, Extreme, caused some users to believe that this category did not include a range, but was the absolute worst departure possible. This was not our intention and we have changed the Extreme category to Extreme to Total in Version 4, Appendix 1.

We strongly recommend that the indicator descriptors in the Evaluation Matrix in Version 4, Appendix 4, for each ecological site be revised and made more specific. This change has been designed to improve consistency among observers. The wording of the "default descriptors" has been retained as "generic descriptors" in nearly all cases. Only minor changes were made to the generic descriptors. These changes clarify the indicators and do not change their interpretation.

In other words, interpretations made with Version 3 will be consistent with those made with Version 4 *provided that the same reference information is used.*

A flow chart under the "Instructions for Using the Rangeland Health Assessment Protocol" section and the Checklist for Rangeland Health Assessment Protocol, Appendix 8, were added to help ensure that all the necessary steps are completed.

Finally, we have added new information, "Quantitative Measures for the 17 Indicators" (Appendix 6), that describes quantitative methods that can be used to generate data to complement this qualitative assessment process.

Table of Contents

Intended Applications

Qualitative assessments of rangeland health provide land managers and technical assistance specialists with a good communication tool for use with the public. Many of these tools have been used successfully for this purpose over the past 100 years. This technique, in association with quantitative monitoring and inventory information, can be used to provide early warnings of resource problems on upland rangelands. Rangelands are defined as "land on which the indigenous vegetation (climax or natural potential) is predominantly grasses, grass-like plants, forbs, or shrubs and is managed as a natural ecosystem. If plants are introduced, they are managed similarly. Rangelands include natural grasslands, savannas, shrublands, many deserts, tundra, alpine communities, marshes, and wet meadows" (Society for Range Management 1999). Also included in this definition are oak and pinyon-juniper woodlands.

The protocol described in this technical reference IS designed to:

- Be used only by knowledgeable, experienced people.
- Provide a preliminary evaluation of soil/site stability, hydrologic function, and biotic integrity (at the ecological site level).
- Be used to communicate fundamental ecological concepts to a wide variety of audiences.
- Improve communication among interest groups by focusing discussion on critical ecosystem properties and processes.
- Select monitoring sites in the development of monitoring programs.
- Provide early warnings of potential problems and opportunities by helping land managers identify areas that are potentially at risk of degradation or where resource problems currently exist.

The protocol is NOT to be used to:

- Identify the cause(s) of resource problems.
- Independently make grazing and other management changes.
- Monitor land or determine trend.
- Independently generate national or regional assessments of rangeland health.

Interpreting Indicators for Rangeland Health has been developed for use by experienced, knowledgeable land managers or technical assistance specialists. This assessment protocol is not intended for use by individuals who do not have experience or knowledge of the rangeland ecological sites they are evaluating. This protocol requires a good understanding of ecological processes, vegetation, and soils for each site to which it is applied. Our research has shown that the quality and consistency of evaluations is improved when two or more individuals (e.g., ecologist and soil scientist) work together. The input of multiple individuals is particularly critical in the development of reference sheets for each ecological site. Development of the reference sheets requires a knowledge of the range of spatial and temporal variability apparent at a particular ecological site.

Introduction

The science of assessing rangelands is changing as concepts and protocols continue to evolve. The concept of rangeland health was advanced as an alternative to range condition (National Research Council 1994). The ecological status concept is currently used by most range professionals as the basis for inventory and assessment. Although the term "health" has been controversial when used in association with natural systems (Wicklum and Davies 1995, Lackey 1998, Rapport et al. 1998, and Smith 1999), this document follows the lead provided by the National Academy of Science (National Research Council 1994).

The National Research Council (NRC 1994) publication, *Rangeland Health: New Methods to Classify, Inventory, and Monitor Rangelands* defined rangeland health as:

> *"The degree to which the integrity of the soil and ecological processes of rangeland ecosystems are maintained."*

In a parallel effort, the Society for Range Management's committee on *Unity in Concepts and Terminology* recommended that rangeland assessments should focus on the maintenance of soil at the site (Task Group on Unity in Concepts and Terminology 1995). A Federal interagency ad hoc committee was established to integrate the concepts of these two groups into the various agencies' rangeland inventories and assessments. This committee refined the above definition to read:

> *"The degree to which the integrity of the soil, vegetation, water, and air, as well as the ecological processes of the rangeland ecosystem are balanced and sustained."*

They defined integrity to mean *"maintenance of the functional attributes characteristic of a locale, including normal variability"* (USDA 1997).

The challenge to scientists and managers is to translate this concept into terms that the public can comprehend, and that resource specialists can use to assist in identifying areas where ecological processes are or are not functioning properly. This document describes a protocol to educate the public and agency personnel on using observable indicators to interpret and assess rangeland health. This protocol relies on the use of a qualitative (non-measurement) procedure to assess the functional status of each indicator.

The use of qualitative assessments is suggested as a fast survey technique to rate site protection indicators, including both plant and soil components (Morgan 1986). The use of qualitative information (e.g., observations) to determine range and soil conditions has a long history of use in land management inventory and monitoring. In some cases, qualitative assessments were used independently, while in other cases they were blended with quantitative measurements. Early procedures that included indicator ratings (e.g., a scorecard approach) included the Interagency Range Survey of 1937, Deming Two-Phase and Parker Three-Step Methods that determined, among other things, site-soil stability and usefulness of forage for livestock grazing (Wagner 1989). The Bureau of Land Management (BLM) also used soil surface factors to determine the erosional status of public lands in the 1970s (USDI 1973). Interagency Technical Reference 1737-9, *Riparian Area Management: Process for Assessing Proper Functioning Condition* (USDI 1993) included a qualitative checklist to assess the proper functioning condition of riparian areas.

This version of *Interpreting Indicators of Rangeland Health* incorporates concepts and materials from previous inventory and monitoring procedures, as well as from the National Research Council's book on Rangeland Health (NRC 1994), and the Society for Range Management's Task Group on Unity in Concepts and Terminology (1995). Development of a landscape ecology approach to assessing rangeland function in Australia also contributed to the understanding of soil processes on North American rangelands and to the interpretations derived from this protocol (Tongway 1994).

The earliest versions of the current procedure were developed concurrently. An interagency technical team led by the BLM developed Version 1a (Pellant 1996). The Natural Resources Conservation Service (NRCS) developed Version 1b, as published in the National Range and Pasture Handbook (USDA 1997). Another interagency team melded these concepts and protocols with the results from numerous field tests of Version 1a (Rasmussen, Pellant, and Pyke 1999) and Version 1b into Version 2. Modifications of Version 2 received peer review and numerous other comments to arrive at the process described in Version 3.

The changes in Version 4 were based on input from a large number of users of Version 3 and are designed to improve the consistency of the application of the process. The most significant modification was the replacement of the Ecological Reference Area Sheet with the Reference Sheet (Appendix 2) (Pyke et al. 2002). The Reference Sheet facilitates consistent application of the process throughout the ecological site by integrating all available sources of data and knowledge to generate a description of the range of expected conditions for each indicator if a site is in the reference state. This includes the associated spatial and temporal variability. It is normally developed for existing ecological sites, but can also be applied to any soil/climate-based land classification system that reflects site potential (see ecological site definition in the Glossary).

Along the way, this procedure has been termed "rapid assessment," "qualitative assessment of rangeland health," and "visualization of rangeland health." This document refers to this procedure as **Interpreting Indicators of Rangeland Health – Version 4**. This version will be revised in the future as science and experience provide additional information on indicators of rangeland health and their assessment.

Relationship to Similarity Index and Trend

The similarity index (range condition) and trend studies have long been used for rangeland assessments. The similarity index can be used as an index of the current plant community in relation to the historic climax plant community, or to a desired plant community that is one of the communities in the reference state for that ecological site (see the section on Concepts: States, Transitions, and Disturbances). Trend is a determination of the direction of change in the current plant community and soils in relation to the community that existed in the past and to the current community along a continuum moving toward a historic climax plant community or some other desired plant community.

This rangeland health assessment is an attempt to look at how well ecological processes on a site are functioning. These three assessment tools (similarity index, trend, and rangeland health assessment) evaluate the rangeland site from different perspectives and are not necessarily correlated (Pierson et al. 2002).

Attributes of Rangeland Health

Ecological processes include the **water cycle** (the capture, storage, and safe release of precipitation), **energy flow** (conversion of sunlight to plant and then animal matter), and **nutrient cycle** (the cycle of nutrients through the physical and biotic components of the environment).

Ecological processes functioning within a normal range of variation support specific plant and animal communities. Direct measures of site integrity and status of ecological processes are difficult or expensive to measure due to the complexity of the processes and their interrelationships. Therefore, biological and physical components are often used as indicators of the functional status of ecological processes and site integrity.

The product of this qualitative assessment is **not** a single rating of rangeland health, but an assessment of three components called attributes (Table 1).

Definitions of these three interrelated attributes are:

Soil/Site Stability
The capacity of an area to limit redistribution and loss of soil resources (including nutrients and organic matter) by wind and water.

Hydrologic Function
The capacity of an area to capture, store, and safely release water from rainfall, run-on, and snowmelt (where relevant), to resist a reduction in this capacity, and to recover this capacity when a reduction does occur.

Biotic Integrity
The capacity of the biotic community to support ecological processes within the normal range of variability expected for the site, to resist a loss in the capacity to support these processes, and to recover this capacity when losses do occur. The biotic community includes plants, animals, and microorganisms occurring both above and below ground.

Each of these three attributes is summarized at the end of the Evaluation Sheet based upon a preponderance of evidence approach using the applicable indicators (Appendix 1). This assessment is preliminary and may be modified with the interpretation of applicable quantitative monitoring and inventory data. Support or rationale for the original rating and any modification of them should be documented on the Evaluation Sheet (Appendix 1).

To reiterate, the protocol described here will produce three ratings, one for each attribute.

Table 1. The three attributes of rangeland health and the rating categories for each attribute.

Soil/Site Stability	Hydrologic Function	Biotic Integrity

Attribute ratings reflect the degree of departure from expected levels for each indicator per the Reference Sheet

Extreme to Total	Moderate to Extreme	Moderate	Slight to Moderate	None to Slight

Concepts

An understanding of the following five concepts is necessary to apply this method.

Landscape Context: Ecological Sites and Watersheds

A landscape is comprised of part or all of one or more watersheds. Several systems have been devised to classify landscapes into similar units for comparisons. *Interpreting Indicators of Rangeland Health* requires the use of a classification system that divides landscapes based on the potential of the land to produce distinctive kinds, amounts, and proportions of vegetation. Soils, climate, and topography together determine this potential. The ecological site concept was developed by the USDA NRCS as one such land classification system. Other site potential-based classification systems can also be used. Where no such system exists (e.g., in Mexico), the method can be locally applied using the best available information. This information is documented in the Reference Sheet (Appendix 2).

Interpreting Indicators of Rangeland Health was designed to be applied at specific locations, known as evaluation areas, in the larger landscape. Evaluators must be able to recognize and correctly identify ecological sites because evaluations are made relative to an ecological site or equivalent. Ecological sites or their equivalents are identified in the field using the factors that determine the site's potential: soils, climate, and topography (USDA 1997).

In addition to ecological site identification, some knowledge of the potential range of spatial variability and of landscape relationships (including characteristics of surrounding areas) is required to interpret evaluations. Since the status of surrounding areas on other ecological sites may influence the evaluation area, we have provided a means of documenting pertinent information about these surrounding areas in the Evaluation Sheet (Appendix 1) and in the Reference Sheet (Appendix 2).

Spatial Variability

An understanding of the potential range of spatial variability both within and among ecological sites is necessary to apply this technique. For example, south-facing slopes are subject to higher evaporation rates and generally have shallower soils than north-facing slopes. Both higher evaporation rates and shallower soil depth result in lower soil moisture availability, increasing bare ground and the potential for rill formation, even on sites that are at or near their potential. Sites that are located lower on the landscape (downslope) may receive runoff water during intense storms or snowmelt. The effect of increased runoff can be positive when the additional water is retained onsite and becomes available for plant growth. Increased runoff can be negative if it results in greater erosion. Microsites that capture wind-driven snow generally have a higher production potential than sites that are typically free of snow, except where snow persists long enough that it significantly limits the length of the growing season. Sometimes these microsite differences are reflected in different ecological sites, but most ecological sites include a broad range of microsites with variable potential.

Landscape Relationships

Some knowledge of landscape relationships is often required to interpret an indicator's departure from that expected for a specific ecological site. Both direct and indirect effects of other landscape units can be important. Direct effects include runoff, erosion, and seed dispersal from surrounding areas. Indirect effects include differences in herbivory, predator-prey, or pathogen-host relationships associated with proximity to water or alternative habitats. For example, recovery or degradation at one location can affect indicators evaluated downslope. While effects of degradation are reflected in the downslope location (e.g., an active gully might be rated as an "extreme to total" departure from the Reference Sheet (Appendix 2), the cause might be increased runoff from another location. Conversely, recovery of plant cover and soil water infiltration capacity in upslope locations can result in reduced water availability for plant growth downslope. These are excellent examples of why it is not recommended that this approach be used alone to assign cause of resource problems. Defining the cause of the gully and the increased production requires a landscape-level analysis and it is possible that the source of the problem is on land controlled by a different manager. Document any off-site influences that affect the evaluation area on the first page of the Evaluation Sheet (Appendix 1).

Spatial Extrapolation

Qualitative watershed, sub-watershed, or sub-basin-scale analyses could be used to generate a map for each of the three attributes based on ecological, site-level evaluations. Appropriate sampling designs are required to aggregate qualitative assessments to larger landscape units. These maps can be overlaid on a soil or ecological site map and used to help identify areas where management interventions are likely to have the greatest effect on runoff, water quality, and other resource concerns. Due to the inherent complexity of many landscapes, many parts of the watershed may need to be mapped as "complexes" in which a single map unit represents several ecological sites and/or a single ecological site that is rated differently in different areas within the map unit (e.g., areas near herbivore watering points may be more degraded than those far from water).

Natural Range of Variability

The biological and physical potential of every location is unique in space and time (Bestelmeyer et al. 2004). To the extent possible, the types and sources of spatial and temporal variability should be described for each indicator on the Reference Sheet (Appendix 2). Sources of spatial variability include soils, climate, natural disturbance events, vegetation communities within the reference state (see States, Transitions, and Disturbances), and topographic position. While all of these are expected to be similar within an ecological site, the quality of evaluations can be improved by recognizing and documenting the expected variation in these sources and documenting how these sources of variation may influence individual indicators on the Reference Sheet.

Plant communities and soils also vary naturally through time. It is expected that bare ground will increase during extended periods of drought, and that woody species and litter cover will be lower following fire. More litter movement and water flow patterns are expected following intense storms in many ecosystems. The temporal range of variability expected within an ecological site should also be reflected in the Reference Sheet (Appendix 2). For example, plant community shifts along pathways within the reference state (Figure 2) should be reflected in the description of the "Plant Functional/Structural Groups" indicator on the Reference Sheet.

Resistance and Resilience

Staying within the natural range of variability depends on the resistance and resilience of the ecosystem. Resistance is the capacity of ecological processes to continue to function with minimal change following a disturbance. Resilience is the capacity of these processes to recover following a disturbance (Figure 1). Resilience can be defined in terms of the rate of recovery, the extent of recovery during a particular period of time, or both (Figure 1).

The resistance and resilience of individual communities vary within a state. Consequently, the specific community that is the least resistant to and/or resilient following a particular disturbance is the one that is most likely to proceed through a transition to another state.

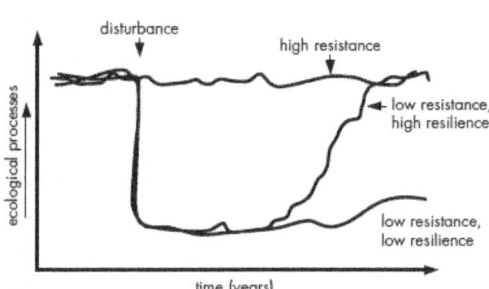

Figure 1. Changes in ecological processes over time following disturbance for systems that vary in resistance and resilience (adapted from Seybold et al. 1999)

Indicators

Ecological processes are difficult to observe or measure in the field due to the complexity of most rangeland ecosystems. Indicators are components of a system whose characteristics (e.g., presence or absence, quantity, distribution) are used as an index of an attribute (e.g., hydrologic function) that is too difficult, inconvenient, or expensive to measure. Just as the Dow Jones Index is used to gauge the strength of a portion of the stock market, different combinations of the 17 indicators are used to gauge soil/site stability, hydrologic function, and biotic integrity.

Indicators have historically been used in rangeland monitoring and resource inventories by land management and technical assistance agencies. These indicators focused on vegetation (e.g., production, composition, density) or soil stability as surrogates for rangeland condition or livestock carrying capacity. Such single attribute assessments are inadequate to determine rangeland health because they do not reflect the complexity of the ecological processes. There is no one indicator of ecosystem health; instead, a suite of key indicators should be used for an assessment (Karr 1992).

Qualitative vs. Quantitative Indicators

Interpreting Indicators of Rangeland Health is based on qualitative indicators. These indicators are appropriate for the objectives described in the "Intended Applications" chapter. Quantitative measurements should be made where it is necessary to document assessments for direct comparisons with other locations, or where monitoring data are required to determine trend.

Quantitative indicators that are correlated with many of the qualitative indicators used in this protocol can be calculated from quantitative measurements (Table 2). More detailed information is included in Appendix 6, Quantitative Measures for the 17 Indicators. In some cases, no equivalent quantitative indicator exists. This reflects the fact that some ecosystem properties are more accurately reflected by qualitative indicators, while others are more effectively measured quantitatively (Rapport 1995). In most cases, the general relationship is similar, but the specific values associated with each departure class vary significantly among ecological sites. For example, rill density for a "none–slight" rating is much higher in badlands ecological sites than in ecological sites located on flat terrain in the central Great Plains of the United States.

The best approach to designing a quantitative monitoring program that is compatible with this qualitative assessment protocol is to select the best quantitative indicators for each of the three *attributes*, rather than selecting an equivalent quantitative indicator for each qualitative indicator. The best quantitative indicators are those that, as a group, are most consistently correlated with the ecosystem functions associated with each of the three attributes. For example, bare ground and soil aggregate stability are both highly correlated with resistance to erosion in most ecological sites, and are therefore good indicators of the "soil/site stability" attribute (Herrick et al. 2005).

Table 2. Key quantitative indicators and measurements relevant to each of the three attributes. Because an appropriate quantitative indicator does not exist for each qualitative indicator, we recommend focusing on selecting the best possible indicators (qualitative and quantitative) for each attribute (for indicator-specific comparisons, please see Appendix 6. References: (1) USDA 1997; (2) Elzinga et al. 1998; and (3) Herrick et al. 2005.

Attribute	Qualitative Assessment Indicators	Key Quantitative Assessment Indicators	Selected Measurements and References
Soil/Site Stability	• Rills • Water flow patterns • Pedestals and/or terracettes • Bare ground • Gullies • Wind-scoured, blowout, and/or depositional areas • Litter movement • Soil surface resistance to erosion • Soil surface loss or degradation • Compaction layer	Bare ground	Line point intercept (2, 3) Point frame (2)
		Proportion of soil surface covered by canopy gaps longer than a defined minimum	Canopy gap intercept (3) Continuous line intercept (2)
		Proportion of soil surface covered by basal gaps longer than a defined minimum	Basal gap intercept (3) Continuous line intercept (2)
		Soil macro-aggregate stability in water	Soil stability kit (3)
Hydrologic Function	• Rills • Water flow patterns • Pedestals and/or terracettes • Bare ground • Gullies • Soil surface resistance to erosion • Soil surface loss or degradation • Plant community composition and distribution relative to infiltration and runoff • Compaction layer • Litter amount	Bare ground	Line point intercept (2, 3) Point frame (2)
		Proportion of soil surface covered by canopy gaps longer than a defined minimum	Canopy gap intercept (3) Continuous line intercept (2)
		Proportion of soil surface covered by basal gaps longer than a defined minimum	Basal gap intercept (3) Continuous line intercept (2)
		Soil macro-aggregate stability in water	Soil stability kit (3)
Biotic Integrity	• Soil surface resistance to erosion • Soil surface loss or degradation • Compaction layer • Functional/structural groups • Plant mortality/decadence • Litter amount • Annual production • Invasive plants • Reproductive capability of perennial plants	Soil macro-aggregate stability in water	Soil stability kit (3)
		Plant canopy (foliar) cover by functional group	Line point intercept (2, 3) Point frame (2)
		Plant basal cover by functional group	Line point intercept (2, 3) Point frame (2)
		Litter cover	Line point intercept (1, 3) Point frame (2)
		Plant production by functional group	Harvest (1) Double sampling (1)
		Invasive plant cover	Line point intercept (1, 3)
		Invasive plant density	Belt transect (2, 3) Quadrats (2)

Vegetation Indicator Consistency: Production, Foliar Cover, and Standing Biomass

The application of this method depends on comparisons to a consistent benchmark. This benchmark varies depending on which indicator is being evaluated, the relationship of certain indicators to production, foliar cover, or biomass, and data collection methods. For *Interpreting Indicators of Rangeland Health*, the Reference Sheet serves as the standard for the 17 indicators. The reference sheet includes information on vegetation composition for several indicators, including but not limited to, functional and structural groups. The evaluation of these indicators is often based on annual production because of the widespread availability of ecological site descriptions, which include production data.

Both standing biomass and foliar cover are correlated with production. However, these relationships vary by species. The relationships between foliar cover, biomass, and production vary among locations and both within and among years in a single location. Dominance rankings of species or functional/structural groups may change depending on which vegetation measure is used. Consequently, uniform substitution of foliar cover or biomass for production is not appropriate. However, foliar cover and biomass can be used as surrogates for production where the relationships are well understood.

Inconsistent comparisons can also arise when different methods are used to quantify or estimate production, foliar cover, or biomass. Annual production estimates include three components: current year's growth present at the time of the evaluation, current year's growth that has been removed by livestock and/or wildlife, and the expected growth (production) during the rest of the year. Expected growth is estimated from standard growth curves. Annual production includes all above-ground production of all species, including stem elongation. Biomass includes all above ground production regardless of the year it was produced.

Foliar cover is simply the proportion of soil surface covered by a vertical projection of a plant canopy. This is effectively the area that is protected from raindrops and the area in shade when the sun is directly overhead. This is the definition used in erosion models. Foliar cover reflects changes in the density of the plant canopy associated with leaf and twig mortality, as well as changes in the size and number of individual plants in a defined area.

Foliar cover measurement or estimates may be based on several approaches including line-point and visual estimates. The line-point method (Elzinga et al. 1998; Herrick et al. 2005) is recommended because it measures the area actually covered by leaves, twigs, and stems, and can be used to assess indicators that are generally more directly related to production, runoff, erosion, and to remote sensing. This method is among the easiest to standardize of all vegetation cover methods and is the preferred method to collect foliar cover for new ecological site descriptions.

Care must be taken in interpreting ecological site descriptions developed prior to 1997 when the NRCS began using foliar cover (USDA 1997) instead of canopy cover in these site descriptions. Canopy cover includes all spaces located within the canopy of an individual plant as "cover," whether or not they were actually protected by a leaf or twig. This resulted in a higher estimate of "cover" particularly for stoloniferous grasses and for shrubs and trees with diffuse canopies and did not reflect foliar cover. Cover data collected for new ecological site descriptions are based on foliar cover.

States, Transitions, and Disturbances

A state includes one or more biological (including soil) communities that occur on a particular ecological site and that are functionally similar with respect to the three attributes (soil/site stability, hydrologic function, and biotic integrity). States are generally distinguished by relatively large differences in plant functional groups, dynamic soil properties, and ecosystem processes, and consequently in vegetation structure, biodiversity, and management requirements. They are also distinguished by their responses to disturbance. A number of different plant communities may be included in a state, and the communities are often connected by community pathways (See Figure 2, Generic state and transition diagram; Bestelmeyer et al. 2002, Stringham et al. 2001).

Shifts between states (solid arrows in Figure 2) are referred to as "transitions." Unlike community pathways (dashed arrows in Figure 2), these "threshold" transitions are not reversible by simply altering the intensity or direction of factors that produced the change. Instead, they may create a physically-altered state, such as an eroded state that has lost part of its A soil horizon. Alternatively, they may require new inputs such as revegetation or shrub removal. Practices such as these, enabling a return to a pre-existing state (USDA 1997), are often expensive to apply. Transitions among states in an ecological site are often caused by a combination of feedback mechanisms that alter soil and plant community dynamics (e.g., Schlesinger et al. 1990). For example, as shrubs replace grasses, runoff and erosion increase from shrub interspaces further reducing soil resource availability for grasses.

The reference state is the state where the functional capacities represented by soil/site stability, hydrologic function, and biotic integrity are performing at a near optimum level under the natural disturbance regime. This state usually includes more than one community, one of which is known as the "historic climax plant community" (see Glossary) and is depicted as one of the communities in the Reference State in Figure 2. Alternatively, some rangeland management or ecology literature (Heady and Child 1994, SRM 1999, Vallentine 1990), recognize one of the communities as the "potential natural plant community." While this technical reference uses the reference state (but not any particular community within the state) as the reference for the rangeland health evaluation, we recognize that managers may choose to manage for communities in another state. In other words, the reference state usually, but not

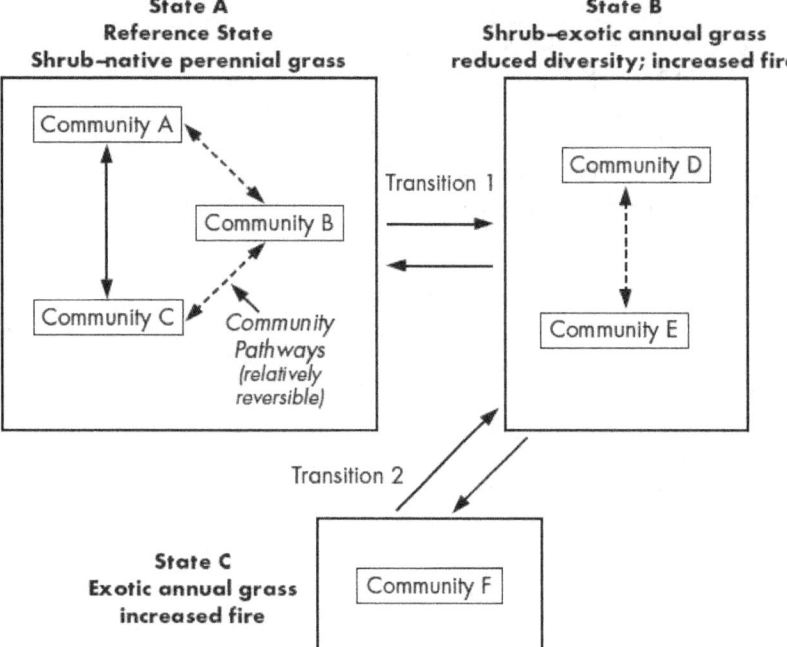

State A	State B
Reference State	Shrub–exotic annual grass
Shrub–native perennial grass	reduced diversity; increased fire

Community A

Community B

Community C

Community Pathways (relatively reversible)

Transition 1

Community D

Community E

Transition 2

State C
Exotic annual grass
increased fire

Community F

Community Pathways	Example
A	Shrubs and native perennial grasses co-dominate (historic climax plant community)
B	Native perennial grasses are dominant; shrubs subdominant
C	Shrubs dominate; perennial grasses subdominant
D	Shrubs dominate; exotic grasses subdominant
E	Exotic grasses dominate; shrubs subdominant
F	Exotic annual grasses dominate

Transitions (relatively non-reversible)

1	Wildfire and introduction of exotic, invasive, annual grasses
2	Repeated wildfires that exceed natural fire-return interval

Figure 2. Generic state and transition diagram. Dashed lines between communities within a state are community pathways; solid lines between states are transitions; and dotted lines between states indicate unlikely reverse transitions (see table with figure for further explanation).

always, includes the manager's desired plant community. However, if sustainability is an objective, the desired plant community will nearly always be found in the reference state (Borman and Pyke 1994).

Some type of disturbance is a natural and necessary part of all ecosystems. Healthy ecosystems are generally both resistant to external disturbances and resilient (able to recover) if external disturbances occur (Pimm 1984). Healthy ecosystems generally allow various communities to fluctuate over time within a state. Transitions rarely occur in response to the natural disturbance regime. However, resistance and resilience alone are insufficient criteria for healthy ecosystems; degraded systems are often highly resistant to change.

Instructions for Using the Rangeland Health Assessment Protocol

A rangeland health assessment provides information on the functioning of ecological processes relative to the reference state for the ecological site or other functionally similar unit for that land area. This assessment provides information that is not available with other methods of evaluation. It gives an indication of the status of the three attributes chosen to represent the health of the "evaluation area" (i.e., the area where the evaluation of the rangeland health attributes occurs). Interest in an evaluation area may be based on concern about current conditions, lack of information on conditions, or public perceptions of conditions.

The following instructions are intended to provide a step-by-step guide for users. Steps are identified along with the document(s) required to complete each step. The action or concept for that step is then explained.

The flow chart in Figure 3 illustrates the entire process and can be used to help decide which steps to complete and the sequence of those steps. Use the Checklist for Rangeland Health Assessment Protocol (Appendix 8) to ensure that you have completed all the required steps.

Step 1. Identify the Evaluation Area, Determine the Soil and Ecological Site (REQUIRED)

Complete page one of the Evaluation Sheet (Appendix 1).

Describe the Evaluation Area

The front of the Evaluation Sheet is used to record information on site location for the assessment and basic site characteristic information for an evaluation area (Appendix 1). The back of this sheet is completed during Step 5.

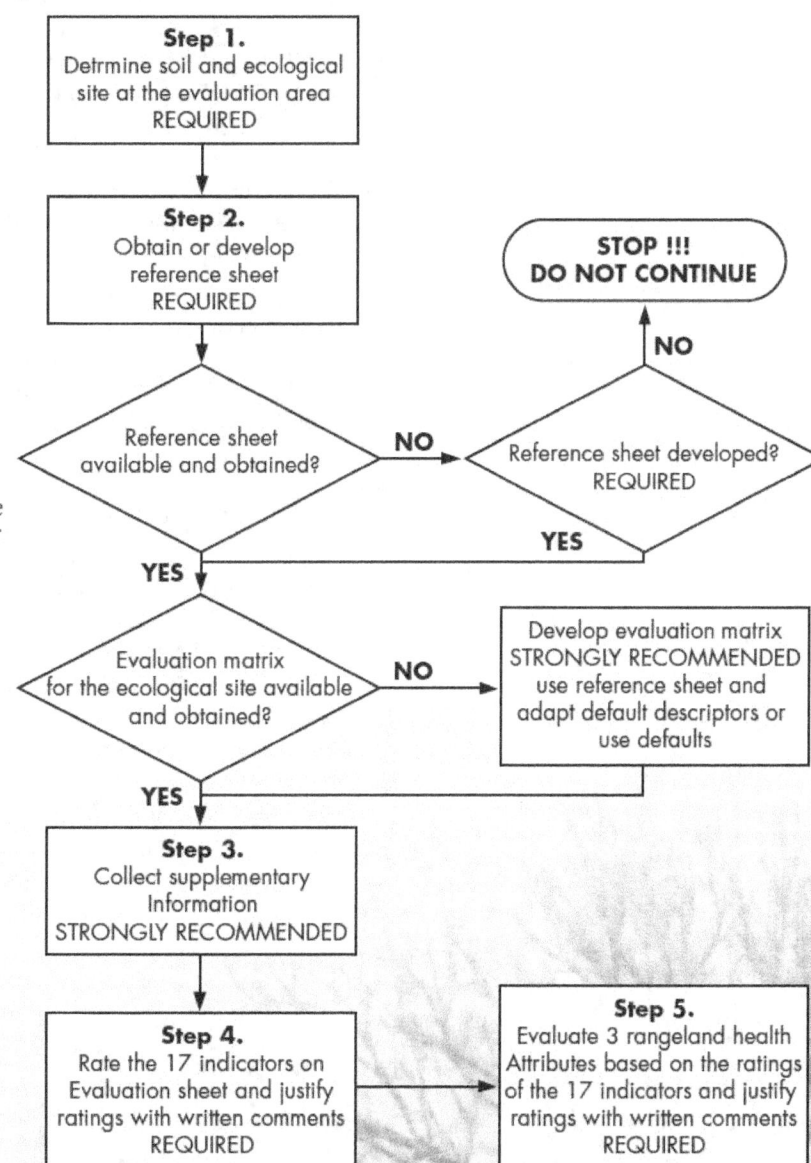

Figure 3. Flowchart for the rangeland health assessment protocol.

The evaluation area should be large enough to accurately evaluate all indicators and should be at least 1/2 to 1 acre in size. An acre is approximately the size of a football field without the end zones. Upon arrival at the location, the evaluator(s) should identify the boundaries of the evaluation area and walk and observe biological and physical characteristics on up to 2 acres of each ecological site in the evaluation area. This enables the evaluator(s) to become familiar with the plant species, soil surface features, and the variability of each ecological site on an evaluation area. A separate evaluation is completed for each ecological site if there is more than one ecological site in the evaluation area unless only one ecological site is of concern in the evaluation area. In this case, ensure that the ecological site boundaries are clearly understood or delineated before conducting the evaluation.

Surrounding features that may affect ecological processes within the evaluation area should also be noted. The topographic position of the evaluation area, adjacent roads, trails, watering points, gullies, timber harvests, and other disturbances can all affect on-site processes. The topographic position should be carefully described with documentation of off-site influences on the evaluation area. There is significant variability in the ecological potential of different ecological sites. This variability is associated with relatively minor differences in landscape position and soils (e.g., differences in aspect, or location at the top versus the bottom of a slope). Landscape position and surrounding features are documented on Page 1 of the Evaluation Sheet (Appendix 1).

Photographs should be taken and included as an attachment to this sheet. Two general view photographs taken in different directions (include some skyline for future point of reference) should be taken along with photographs that illustrate important indicator values or anomalies. Time, date, orientation, and location of the photo should be recorded.

Determine the Soil and Ecological Site

Each ecological site within the evaluation area should be verified by matching the evaluation area to the appropriate ecological site description and soils. The best way to confirm the soil classification, and thus the ecological site, is to dig several shallow pits to verify that the soil profile characteristics are consistent with those of the soils listed in the ecological site description. Soil surveys (which include soil maps and other useful information) should also be consulted if the soil information in the ecological site description is inadequate to correlate soils to the appropriate ecological site description. The evaluator(s) should review the ecological site description for consistency with the soils and vegetation found on the evaluation area.

Always use the Reference Sheet corresponding to the appropriate ecological site. On-site soil description and comparison with soils listed or described in the ecological site description should be completed even when a soil map is available. Soil maps should only be used to help predict soils (and therefore ecological sites) that might be found in the evaluation area. This is because many soil map units are comprised of more than one soil. In addition, soil "inclusions" or soils representing a relatively small proportion of each map unit are found in the vast majority of soil map units in the United States. Inclusions may or may not be listed in the soil survey. Each soil in a map unit may belong to a different ecological site. Finally, even single soil series can belong to more than one ecological site if the functionally significant properties vary significantly within the same soil series. Surface texture and slope are examples of functionally significant properties.

Document the soil profile information in the soil/site identification section of the front page of the Evaluation Sheet (Appendix 1). Soil features that are important to soil/plant/air/water relationships are also included whether or not they are required for soil identification. Soil texture for each horizon, and soil depth, or depth to horizons which may restrict water movement or root growth (e.g., calcic or sodic) or hold more water (e.g., argillic), and other soil features which are important to soil/plant/air/water relationships need to be identified in order to interpret the indicators. Including a soil scientist or resource specialist familiar with soil classifications in this phase of the evaluation is recommended.

Actions to Take if Soil and/or Ecological Site Information Are Not Available

In areas where soil surveys are unavailable or inadequate, aerial photographs, topographic maps, geologic maps, and local weather records can often be used to help decide which ecological site description from adjacent surveyed areas is most appropriate (see Table 3). Where ecological site descriptions are unavailable, these resources can sometimes be used to identify relevant ecological site descriptions that have been developed for similar areas in the region. Vegetation information may be available from other sources, such as habitat-type descriptions, long-term monitoring studies, and other inventory data. If possible, enlist the service of a soil scientist to assist the evaluator(s) in making the initial soil/site correlations.

The process used to conduct the evaluation without the required soils and ecological site information should be clearly documented by the team on the Evaluation Sheet (Appendix 1).

Table 3. Information sources useful in completing Part I of the Evaluation Sheet (Appendix 1) and development of Reference Sheets (Appendix 2). For an updated version of this form, see http://usda-ars.nmsu.edu/JER/Monit_Assess/monitoring.htm.

Resources	Sources
Aerial photos	• USGS at http://edcsns17.cr.usgs.gov/EarthExplorer • Companies selling USGS photos at http://geography.usgs.gov/partners/viewonline.html • http://mapping.usgs.gov/esic/esic_index.html, http://ask.usgs.gov/sources.html, or call 1-888-ASK-USGS (1-888-275-8747). Images newer than 1996 can be obtained from the National Aerial Photography Program (NAPP) and National High Altitude Photography (NHAP), and are searchable on Earth Explorer at http://edcsns17.cr.usgs.gov/EarthExplorer • USDA Sales Branch, USDA FSA APFO, 2222 West 2300 South, Salt Lake City, Utah, 84119-2020, or 801-975-3503, or http://www.apfo.usda.gov/Ordering%20Imagery.htm
Aerial photos: Digital Orthophoto Quarter Quadrangle (DOQQ)	• An aerial photograph that has been digitized (scanned into a computer) and georectified, giving it all the properties of a map. DOQQs are helpful when using GIS technology to stratify landscapes • USGS or its business partners at http://rockyweb.cr.usgs.gov/acis-bin/querypartner.cgi • USDA NRCS at http://www.ncgc.nrcs.usda.gov/products/datasets/index.html
Topographic maps	• 7.5 minute USGS topographic maps at http://topomaps.usgs.gov • Other topographic maps can be purchased in hard copy or CD from USGS or its business partners at http://geography.usgs.gov/www/partners/bpprod.html
Digital Raster Graphic (DRG)	• A scanned USGS topographic map that has been digitized (scanned into a computer) and georectified, ready for GIS applications • USGS or its business partners at http://topomaps.usgs.gov/drg
Soil surveys and maps	• Visit the local NRCS office (look under United States Government, Department of Agriculture, USDA Natural Resources Conservation Service in the blue pages of the phone book), or check the NRCS website (http://soils.usda.gov/survey) to obtain a copy of a soil survey for the county of interest. • STATSGO (State Soil Geographic Database) map coverage (1:250,000) is available for most areas. SSURGO (1:24,000) maps are in the process of being digitized. Hard copies are available hrough local NRCS offices. • Visit the local USFS office to obtain a Terrestrial Ecosystem Survey for the area of interest. Some offices may have this data available in digital form.
Vegetation inventory data	• BLM land: Soil Vegetation Inventory Method (SVIM) maps. These are maps of field-collected vegetation inventory data. Some offices may have this data available in GIS form. • Private land: NRCS status maps and Natural Resources Inventory data are found at http://www.nrcs.usda.gov/technical/dataresources or http://www.nrcs.usda.gov/technical/land
General maps	• BLM land status maps (look under United States Government, Department of the Interior, Bureau of Land Management, in the blue pages of the phone book)
Species lists	• USFS, BLM, and NRCS offices (especially old monitoring records) • NRCS lists of plants: http://www.nrcs.usda.gov/technical/dataresources • See ecological site descriptions (NRCS) below. • Look up your local chapter of the Native Plant Society at http://www.nanps.org/about/frame.shtml • Plants national database at http://plants.usda.gov
Ecological (range) site descriptions	• Local NRCS office (ask for the "range site handbook" or go to http://esis.sc.egov.usda.gov). • Some revised descriptions may not yet be on the Web.
Geologic maps	• USGS Geologic Maps at http://ngmdb.usgs.gov
Invasive species	• NRCS at http://plants.usda.gov/cgi_bin/topics.cgi?earl=noxious.cgi

Step 2. Obtain or Develop the Reference Sheet (REQUIRED) and the Corresponding Evaluation Matrix (STRONGLY RECOMMENDED)

Obtain a Reference Sheet (Appendix 2) (REQUIRED)

The Reference Sheet describes the status of each indicator for the reference state (see "States, Transitions, and Disturbances" in the Concepts section). It serves as the primary reference for the evaluation. The reference sheet describes a range for each indicator based on expected spatial and temporal variability within each ecological site (or equivalent).

Reference Sheets are currently being incorporated into ecological site descriptions. If the ecological site description does not include this information, ask the person responsible for maintaining ecological site descriptions in the state (usually the NRCS State Rangeland Management Specialist) if a draft is available.

If an ecological site description does not exist, additional expertise will be required to develop the Reference Sheet (see the Instructions for Reference Sheet Development). If expertise or time is limited, the rangeland health evaluation should not proceed. It is not possible to properly conduct an evaluation without a Reference Sheet. Development of the Reference Sheet will require as much or more expertise than is required to conduct the evaluation. Memory of a similar site, professional opinion of what the site could be, visits to reference areas, or reviews of old range or ecological site descriptions that do not contain reference sheets are not adequate substitutes for a properly developed Reference Sheet. However, all of these information sources can be used in the development of the Reference Sheet.

Instructions for Reference Sheet Development

Before beginning development, be sure to check with the NRCS State Rangeland Management Specialist to find out if a final or draft Reference Sheet is available. If a draft is available, but has not been finalized, you may use it and provide comments or suggest modifications to the NRCS State Rangeland Management Specialist. If no Reference Sheet exists, develop one using the following protocol and send it to the NRCS State Rangeland Management Specialist.

1. Assemble a diverse group of experts with extensive knowledge of the ecological site.
Individuals should be included who have long-term knowledge of the variability and dynamics of the ecological site, in addition to rangeland professionals who understand general soil-climate-vegetation relationships.

2. Provide this group of experts with all available sources of information.
Information should include relevant scientific literature and data from potential reference areas, including data used to support the ecological site descriptions.

3. Define the functional/structural groups for the ecological site (or equivalent).
Use the Functional/Structural Groups Sheet (Appendix 3) to define the functional/ structural groups and the species associated with each group. This sheet is used to group species into life form/functional/structural categories, to determine the potential dominance rating (complete the "potential" column on this sheet) expected among these groups within the reference state, and to aid in the rating of Indicator 12, Functional/Structural Groups. It is important to have a good understanding of the characteristics that may define functional groups. These characteristics include, but are not limited to, lifeform (e.g., tree, shrub, sub-shrub, grass, forb, moss, lichen, cyanobacteria), nitrogen fixation potential, rooting depth, morphology, photosynthetic pathways (warm vs. cool season plants), and whether or not the plants are native to the ecological site. Examples of functional/ structural groups, and more information on the determination of these groups, may be found in the narrative for Indicator 12 (Functional/Structural Groups) in Step 4.

The dominance rating for each functional/structural group included in the Functional/Structural Groups Sheet and the Reference Sheet are based on a description of dominant or subdominant based on percent composition (relative production, biomass, or cover per unit area). Each Functional/Structural Group should be identified on the Reference Sheet as either dominant, subdominant, or other for Indicator 12. Then on the optional Functional/Structural Groups Sheet, each Functional/Structural Group is placed into one of four categories (dominant, subdominant, minor, or trace) in the Potential column (indicating the expected dominance rating for the reference state). This column should correspond with the ratings given on Indicator 12 on the Reference Sheet. Later at an evaluation area, the observers can complete the actual dominance rating (complete the "Actual" column on the worksheet) to aid in rating indicators on the evaluation sheet.

When evaluating a site, several of the 17 indicators require an interpretation regarding changes in this dominance rating for the Functional/Structural Groups, or in the numbers of species within these Functional/Structural Groups. It is important to use the same measure of dominance in the evaluation as was used in the Reference Sheet. For example, if percent of composition based on production was used because the ecological site description used it, then percent of composition by production should be the variable used by the observer when making the evaluation of these indicators.

4. Visit one or more ecological reference areas (optional).
A visit to one or more potential ecological reference areas (ERAs) can be a useful source of additional information for the Reference Sheet. It can also be used by evaluators to improve their ability to recognize the indicators in the field and to "field check" the descriptors developed in the office.

An ERA is a landscape unit in which ecological processes are functioning within a normal range of variability and the plant communities have adequate resistance to and resiliency from most disturbances. An

ERA is the visual representation of the characteristics and variability of the components found in the ecological site description. These areas do not need to be pristine, historically unused lands (e.g., climax plant communities or relict areas).

A number of different plant communities have the potential to meet these criteria. Species composition does not have to match the ecological site description. However, the functional and structural groups must closely match the potential depicted in the ecological site description. Care must be taken in using the ecological site description or ERA as a reference when disturbances have occurred. For example, if a fire occurred 5 years ago in the evaluation area, the ERA should reflect the effects of a recent burn. To obtain this understanding, the evaluator(s) should review appropriate rangeland ecological site (range site) descriptions and select and use appropriate ERAs for training and evaluation purposes.

Sources to assist in the selection of potential ERAs include:

- Ecological site descriptions
- Soil surveys
- Topographic maps
- Vegetation inventories
- Maps showing locations of Research Natural Areas, Wilderness Study Areas, or other protected (large exclosures)/special management areas
- Historical records and photographs
- Records of well-managed rangelands where grazing use has maintained ecological processes and the plant community in a proper functioning state; grazing use pattern maps are helpful in identifying these areas.

This concept is similar to that proposed by the Western Regional Coordinating Committee-40 on Rangeland Research for using well-managed rangelands and appropriate relict areas as benchmarks for assessments (West et al. 1994). The concept of ERAs is also an integral component in the development of ecological site descriptions.

At each ERA, the evaluator(s) should take photographs, collect relevant quantitative data (see Appendix 6), describe the status of each indicator, and record whether or not you believe that it reflects reference conditions (based on all other available information). The area should be used as a reference only for indicators that would be rated as None to Slight based on the final version of the Reference Sheet. The Reference Sheet is the ultimate standard against which all areas, including "reference" areas, are evaluated.

Where possible, a number of ERAs that represent the range of variability in the reference state should be visited (see Figure 2 in States, Transitions, and Disturbances in the Concepts section).

5. Describe the status of each indicator in the reference state (Corresponds to the None-to-Slight departure from the expected for the site in the Evaluation Matrix). These descriptors should be quantitative whenever possible and must include expected ranges based on natural disturbance regimes (e.g., insect outbreaks, wildfires, native herbivore influence), weather, and spatial variability for all plant communities included in the reference state for the ecological site (see Appendix 2, Reference Sheet, Standard Example). Ecological sites include a range of soils with similar, but not identical, characteristics. In many cases, the effects of within-site variability in factors such as soil texture, depth, aspect, slope, and shape of slope on the indicator must be described. For example, concave areas within an ecological site are more likely to receive run-on water and therefore production potential is higher. For additional guidance, please see Landscape Context and Natural Range of Variability in the Concepts section.

Where available, data or other information used to support the descriptor should be cited (e.g., from the ecological site description). Be sure to specify whether composition estimates are based on current year's production, cover produced during the current year, or biomass (check appropriate box at top of sheet).

Obtain the Evaluation Matrix (Appendix 4) for the Ecological Site (or Equivalent Unit) (STRONGLY RECOMMENDED)

The Evaluation Matrix includes detailed descriptions for each of the five departure categories for each indicator.

The Evaluation Matrix includes five descriptors for each indicator which reflect the range of departure from what is expected for the site: None to Slight, Slight to Moderate, Moderate, Moderate to Extreme, and Extreme to Total. The descriptor for "None to Slight" comes directly from the Reference Sheet (Appendix 2) and reflects the range of variation of the indicator in the reference state. The descriptors for the other four classes are derived from the Reference Sheet and the generic descriptors included in Appendix 4 by the team developing the Evaluation Matrix.

A unique Evaluation Matrix will eventually be included in each ecological site description. Until this information is available, generic descriptors may be used or adapted to better reflect current knowledge. To maintain consistency of assessments on specific ecological sites, one of the following options MUST be applied:

- Add notes to the generic descriptors (Appendix 4) to clarify how each descriptor is interpreted for the site.

   OR

- Create an ecological site-specific Evaluation Matrix (see the following instructions for Evaluation Matrix Development).

This Evaluation Matrix (Appendix 4) should be used for subsequent evaluations on the **same ecological site** and any changes should be forwarded to the person responsible for maintaining ecological site descriptions in the State (usually the NRCS State Rangeland Management Specialist). This will ensure that these modifications will be considered in ongoing revisions of ecological site descriptions.

Instructions for Evaluation Matrix Development

1. For each indicator, copy a summary of the reference sheet description into the None-to-Slight box. This summary will include a range of values that accounts for the spatial and temporal variability expected within an ecological site.

2. Write a descriptor for "Extreme" or modify the generic descriptor. Extreme is defined as Extreme to Total (e.g., 100 percent or complete) departure from the narrative found in the None-to-Slight box. The range included in this departure category varies among ecological sites and is relative to disturbance events. For example, in a tallgrass prairie site (40" precipitation), Extreme departure for bare ground might include 30–100 percent bare ground except immediately following fire or an extended drought. In a non-gravelly Mojave Desert site (less than 6" precipitation), Extreme to Total departure might range from 95–100 percent bare ground. As for the None-to-Slight descriptor, this will include a range of values that accounts for the spatial and temporal variability expected within an ecological site.

3. Write or modify descriptors for Slight to Moderate, Moderate, and Moderate to Extreme.

Indicators of soil/site stability are particularly likely to require these changes due to the inherently higher erosion potential on certain ecological sites. An Evaluation Matrix (Appendix 4) example follows (Table 4) of a modified and expanded bare ground descriptor narrative for the Limy ecological site in MLRA 42 (south-central New Mexico). Similar changes should be made for other indicators.

Table 4. Example of a revised descriptor for the bare ground indicator.

	Departure from Reference Sheet				
Indicator	Extreme to Total	Moderate to Extreme	Moderate	Slight to Moderate	None to Slight
4. Bare ground	Greater than 75% bare ground with entire area connected. Only occasional areas where ground cover is contiguous, mostly patchy and sparse.	60-75% bare ground. Bare patches are large (>24" diameter) and connected. Surface disturbance areas becoming connected to one another. Connectivity of bare ground broken occasionally by contiguous ground cover.	45-60% bare ground with much connectivity especially associated with surface disturbance. Individual bare spaces are large and dominate the area.	30-45% bare ground. Bare spaces greater than 12" diameter and rarely connected. Bare areas associated with surface disturbance are larger (> 15") and may be connected to other bare patches.	**Reference Sheet:** 20-30% bare ground; bare patches should be less than 8-10" diameter and not connected; occasional 12" patches associated w/shrubs. Larger bare patches also associated with ant mounds and small mammal disturbances.
Generic Descriptor	Much higher than expected for the site. Bare areas are large and generally connected.	Moderate to much higher than expected for the site. Bare areas are large and occasionally connected.	Moderately higher than expected for the site. Bare areas are of moderate size and sporadically connected.	Slightly to moderately higher than expected for the site. Bare areas are small and rarely connected.	Amount and size of bare areas match that expected for the site.

Step 3. Collect Supplementary Information (STRONGLY RECOMMENDED)

Supplementary information is collected to improve the evaluators' ability to make an accurate evaluation. There are four general types of supplementary information: (1) spatial and temporal variability, including factors affecting the variability; (2) information from relevant ecological reference areas; (3) functional/ structural groups; and (4) quantitative cover and composition data for the evaluation site.

Spatial and Temporal Variability

The Reference Sheet and Evaluation Matrix describe the range of variability expected to occur in an ecological site (or equivalent geographic unit). There is significant spatial variability in site potential within ecological sites depending on soils, slope, aspect, and landscape position. For example, for an ecological site that includes slopes ranging from 5-15 percent, water flow patterns are expected to be more pronounced on steeper slopes. Documenting these relatively static properties on the first page of the Evaluation Sheet (Appendix 1) can help increase the accuracy of the evaluation.

Temporal variability is even greater than spatial variability in most ecological sites. The season, time since the last storm or fire, and recent precipitation are just a few of the factors that can affect current site potential. These factors can also be documented on the Evaluation Sheet and used to increase evaluation accuracy.

Ecological Reference Areas

Ecological reference areas (see Step 2), where available, can help by providing a visual representation of the expected status of each indicator at the time of the evaluation. Quantitative data (see Table 5) can also be used to supplement the information in the Reference Sheet. Ecological reference areas should be functioning at least as well as described in the Reference Sheet with respect to soil/site stability, hydrologic function, and biotic integrity.

Evaluators need to examine ecological reference areas in the same year and season as the evaluation area, since weather during that year may affect the rating of indicators. However, ecological reference areas may be located in different watersheds within the geographic region as long as the current year's weather has been similar between locations. See the "Reference Sheet Development" section in Step 2 for more information on ecological reference areas.

Functional/Structural Groups Sheet

The Functional/Structural Groups Sheet (part of which was developed as part of Step 2) can be used to directly compare potential (Step 2) and actual (fill in the "Actual" column of the Functional/Structural Groups Sheet) relative dominance (composition) of the functional/ structural groups.

Quantitative Data

Table 5 shows how quantitative vegetation and soil data can be used to support the indicator evaluation. For additional quantitative indicators, see Table 2 and Appendix 6.

Table 5. Quantitative indicators for selected indicators

	4. Bare ground	8. Soil surface resistance to erosion	10. Plant community composition and distribution relative to infiltration and runoff	12. Functional/ structural groups	13. Plant mortality and decadence	14. Litter amount	15. Annual production	16. Invasive plants
Indicator								
Information	Bare ground % Size of inter-canopy gaps	Stability of soil surface in water	Functional group composition (relative dominance)	Functional group composition (relative dominance)	Percentage of point species intercepts that are dead	Litter cover (litter depth and density also required to calculate amount but are rarely collected)	Total annual production	Relative dominance
Recommended methods*	Line point Gap intercept	Stability kit	Production OR Line point	Production OR Line point	Line point	Line point (for litter cover)	Production	Production OR Line point Belt transect (for low cover)

* Described in the "Monitoring Manual for Grassland, Shrubland and Savanna Ecosystems" (printed copies available from University of Arizona Press in pdf format at http://usda-ars.nmsu.edu/JER/Monit_Assess/monitoring.htm.

Step 4. Rate the 17 Indicators on the Evaluation Sheet (REQUIRED)

Complete the Evaluation Sheet (Appendix 1, back page) using the Evaluation Matrix (Appendix 4).

Evaluators select the category descriptor (i.e., narrative) on the Evaluation Matrix (Appendix 4) that most closely describes each indicator and records it on the Evaluation Sheet, Page 2. The rating for each indicator in the evaluation area is based on that indicator's degree of departure from the Reference Sheet (Appendix 2). This is based on the ecological site description and other information, including expert knowledge of structure, function, and dynamics of ecological reference areas and other areas within the ecological site (see Step 2). The Reference Sheet reflects the range of variability expected for soils and plant communities in the reference state. The Functional/Structural Groups worksheet (Appendix 3) is also useful in evaluating several indicators. For other relevant quantitative indicators, see Table 2 in the Concepts section.

Narrative descriptions in the Evaluation Matrix are intended to aid in the determination of the degree of departure. The narrative descriptors for each indicator form a relative scale from "Extreme to Total" to "None to Slight." Not all indicator descriptors will match what is observed, requiring a "best fit" approach when making ratings. The rating for each indicator should be supported by comments in the space provided by each indicator rating. In some instances, there may be no evidence of the indicator on the evaluation area. Those indicators are rated "None to Slight."

When making an assessment, the effects of natural disturbances (e.g., drought, fire) should be considered. For example, if a fire occurred 5 years ago in the area being assessed, reduced shrub (e.g., sagebrush) cover is not necessarily an indication of lack of biotic integrity if natural processes alone are sufficient to allow recovery of the original plant community. Both the pre- and post-fire plant community are in the same reference state (see Figure 2, generic state and transition diagram, in the Concepts section). Comments on wildfire return intervals (expected and current) must be documented in the comments section on this sheet.

Important: Be sure to specify whether composition estimates are based on current year's production, cover produced during the current year, or biomass, and check the appropriate box at top of the sheet).

Indicators

Descriptions of each indicator are provided in the following sections. Color photographs of the indicators are located in Appendix 5. Additional information on many of the soil-related indicators can be found in the Rangeland Soil Quality Information Sheets (NRCS Soil Quality Institute et al.2002; http://soils.usda.gov/sqi/soil_quality/land_management/range.html).

1. Rills

Rills (small erosional rivulets) are generally linear and do not necessarily follow the microtopography that flow patterns do. They are formed through complex interactions between raindrops, overland flow, and the characteristics of the soil surface (Bryan 1987). The potential for rills increases as the degree of disturbance (loss of cover) and slope increases. Some soils have a greater potential for rill formation than others (Bryan 1987, Quansah 1985). Therefore, it is important to establish the degree of natural versus accelerated rill formation by interpretations made from the soil survey, rangeland ecological site description, and the ecological reference area. Generally, concentrated flow erosional processes are accelerated when the distance between rills decreases and the depth and width of rills increase (Morgan 1986, Bryan 1987).

2. Water Flow Patterns

Flow patterns are the path that water takes (i.e., accumulates) as it moves across the soil surface during overland flow. Overland flow will occur during rainstorms or snowmelt when a surface crust impedes water infiltration, or the infiltration capacity is exceeded. These patterns are generally evidenced by litter, soil or gravel redistribution, or pedestalling of vegetation or stones that break the flow of water (Morgan 1986). Interrill erosion caused by overland flow has been identified as the dominant sediment transport mechanism on rangelands (Tiscareno-Lopez et al. 1993). Water flow patterns are controlled in length and coverage by the number and kinds of obstructions to water flow provided by basal intercepts of living or dead plants, biological crust, persistent litter, or rocks. They are rarely continuous, and appear and disappear as the slope and microtopography of the slope changes. Shorter flow patterns facilitate infiltration by helping to pond water in depositional areas, thereby increasing the time for water to soak into the soil.

Generally, as slope increases and ground cover decreases, flow patterns increase (Morgan 1986). Soils with inherently low infiltration capacity may have a large number of natural flow patterns.

3. Pedestals and/or Terracettes

Pedestals and terracettes are important indicators of the movement of soil by water and/or by wind (Anderson 1974, Morgan 1986, Satterlund and Adams 1992, Hudson 1993). Pedestals are rocks or plants that appear elevated as a result of soil loss by wind or water erosion. Pedestals can also be caused by non-erosional processes, such as frost heaving or through soil or litter deposition on and around plants (Hudson 1993). Thus, it is important to distinguish and not include this type of pedestalling as an indication of erosional processes.

Terracettes are benches of soil deposition behind obstacles caused by water movement (not wind). As the degree of soil movement by water increases, terracettes become higher and more numerous and the area of soil deposition becomes larger. Terracettes caused by livestock or wildlife movements on hillsides are not considered erosional terracettes, thus they are not assessed in this protocol. However, these terracettes can affect erosion by concentrating water flow and/or changing infiltration. These effects are recorded with the appropriate indicators (e.g., water flow patterns, compaction layer, and soil surface loss and degradation).

4. Bare Ground

Bare ground is exposed mineral or organic soil that is susceptible to raindrop splash erosion, the initial form of most water-related erosion (Morgan 1986). It is the remaining ground cover after accounting for ground surface covered by vegetation (basal and canopy (foliar) cover), litter, standing dead vegetation, gravel/rock, and visible biological crust (e.g., lichen, mosses, algae) (Weltz, et al. 1998).

The amount and distribution of bare ground is one of the most important contributors to site stability relative to the site potential; therefore, it is a direct indication of site susceptibility to accelerated wind or water erosion (Smith and Wischmeier 1962, Morgan 1986, Benkobi, et al. 1993, Blackburn and Pierson 1994, Pierson et al. 1994, Gutierrez and Hernandez 1996, Cerda 1999). In general, a site with bare soil present in a few large patches will be less stable than a site with the same ground cover percentage in which the bare soil is distributed in many small patches, especially if these patches are unconnected (Gould 1982, Spaeth et al. 1994, Puigdefabregas and Sanchez 1996).

The amount of bare ground can vary seasonally, depending on impacts on vegetation canopy (foliar) cover (e.g., herbivore utilization), and litter amount (e.g., trampling loss), and can vary annually relative to weather (e.g., drought, above average precipitation) (Gutierrez and Hernandez 1996, Anderson 1974). Current and past climate must be considered in determining the adequacy of current cover in protecting the site against the potential for accelerated erosion.

5. Gullies

A gully is a channel that has been cut into the soil by moving water. Gullies generally follow natural drainages and are caused by accelerated water flow and the resulting downcutting of soil. Gullies are a natural feature of some landscapes and ecological sites, while on others management actions (e.g., excessive grazing, recreation vehicles, or road drainages) may cause gullies to form or expand (Morgan 1986). In gullies, water flow is concentrated but intermittent. Gullies can be caused by resource problems offsite (document this on the Evaluation Sheet, Appendix 2), but still affect the site function on the evaluation area.

Gullies may be assessed by observing the numbers of gullies in an area and/or assessing the severity of erosion on individual gullies. General signs of active erosion, (e.g., incised sides along a gully) are indicative of a current erosional problem, while a healing gully is characterized by rounded banks, vegetation growing in the bottom and on the sides (Anderson 1974), and a reduction in gully depth (Martin and Morton 1993). Active headcuts may be a sign of accelerated erosion in a gully even if the rest of the gully is showing signs of healing (Morgan 1986).

6. Wind-Scoured, Blowout, and/or Depositional Areas

Accelerated wind erosion, on an otherwise stable soil, increases as the surface crust (i.e., either physical, chemical, or biological crust) is worn by disturbance or abrasion. Physical crusts are extremely important in protecting the soil surface from wind erosion on many rangelands with low canopy (foliar) cover. The exposed soil beneath these surface crusts is often weakly consolidated and vulnerable to movement via wind (Chepil and Woodruff 1963). As wind velocity increases, soil particles begin bouncing against each other in the saltation process. This abrasion leads to suspension of fine particles into the wind stream where they may be transported off the site (Chepil 1945, Gillette, et al. 1972, Gillette, et al. 1974, Gillette and Walker 1977, Hagen 1984).

Wind erosion is reflected by wind-scoured or blowout areas where the finer particles of the topsoil have blown away, sometimes leaving residual gravel, rock, or exposed roots on the soil surface (Anderson 1974). They are generally found in interspace areas with a close correlation between soil cover/bare patch size, soil texture, and degree of accelerated erosion (Morgan 1986).

Deposition of suspended soil particles is often associated with vegetation that provides roughness to slow the wind velocity and allow soil particles to settle from the wind stream. The taller the vegetation, the greater the deposition rate (Pye 1987); thus shrubs and trees in rangeland ecosystems are likely sinks for deposition (e.g., mesquite dunes, Gibbens et al. 1983, Hennessey et al. 1983). The soil removed from wind-scoured depressions is redistributed to accumulation areas (e.g., eolian deposits), which increase in size and area of coverage as the degree of wind erosion increases (Anderson 1974).

Like water erosion, wind deposited soil particles can originate from offsite but affect the function of the site by modifying soil surface texture (Hennessey et al. 1986, Morin and Van Winkel 1996). The changes in texture will influence the site's hydrologic function. Even when soil particles originate from offsite, they can have detrimental effects on plants at the depositional site.

7. Litter Movement

The degree and amount of litter (i.e., dead plant material that is in contact with the soil surface) movement is an indicator of the degree of wind and/or water erosion. The redistribution of litter within a small area on a site is indicative of less erosion, whereas the movement of litter offsite is an indication of more severe erosion. In a study in the Edwards Plateau in Texas, litter accumulation was shown to be the variable most closely correlated with interrill erosion. The same study showed that litter of bunchgrasses represented significant obstructions to runoff, thereby causing sediment transport capacity to be reduced and a portion of the sediment to be deposited (Thurow, et al. 1988a).

The inherent capacity for litter movement on a soil is a function of its slope and geomorphic stability. For example, alluvial fans and flood plains are active surfaces over which water and sediments are moved in response to major storm events. The amount of litter movement varies from large to small depending on the amount of bare space typical of the plant community and the intensity of the storm.

The size of litter moved by wind or water is also an indicator of the degree of litter redistribution. In general, the greater distance that litter is moved from its point of origin and the larger the size and/or amount of litter moved, the more the site is being influenced by erosional processes.

8. Soil Surface Resistance to Erosion

This indicator assesses the resistance of the surface of the soil to erosion. Resistance depends on soil stability and on the spatial variability in soil stability relative to vegetation and microtopographic features. The stability of the soil surface is key to this indicator (Morgan 1986). Soil surfaces may be stabilized by soil organic matter which has been fully incorporated into aggregates at the soil surface, adhesion of decomposing organic matter to the soil surface, and biological crusts. The presence of one or more of these factors is a good indicator of soil surface resistance to erosion (Blackburn et al. 1992, Pierson et al. 1994).

Soil surface resistance to erosion in arid and semi-arid ecosystems is often higher under plant canopies than in interspaces. Where the site potential is different under plant canopies, both canopy and interspace values should be reported on the Reference Sheet (Appendix 2).

When soil surface resistance is high, soil erosion may be minimal even under rainfall intensities of over 5 inches/hour (Goff, et al. 1993). Conversely, the presence of highly erodible materials at the soil surface can dramatically increase soil erosion by water, even when there is high vegetative cover (Morgan et al. 1997), and by wind when vegetative cover is removed (Fryrear et al.1994, Belnap and Gillette 1998).

In areas with low vegetative cover, soil stability in plant interspaces is more important than stability under plants. Similarly, where pedestals have formed along flow paths, the soil at the edge of the pedestal will be subjected to more intense forces during overland flow than soil which is topographically above the flow path.

Another good indicator is the resistance of soil surface fragments to breakdown when placed in water. For a simple test, use the tip of a knife to remove several small (maximum 1/4 inch diameter, 1/8 inch deep) soil surface fragments from beneath plants, interspaces, and any other areas which might differ in soil stability. Place each in a separate bottlecap filled with water. Fragments with low stability will appear to lose their structure or "melt" within 30 seconds. Fragments with extremely low stability will "melt" immediately upon contact with the water and the water will become cloudy as the soil particles disperse. Fragments with moderate stability will appear to retain their integrity until the water in the bottlecap is agitated or gently swirled. Highly stable aggregates will retain their shape, even when agitated indefinitely. For multiple samples, or where more precision is desired, a simple soil stability kit can be used to generate a rating from one (unstable) to six (stable) (Herrick et al. 2001) (Appendix 7). This indicator is more highly correlated with water erosion (Blackburn and Pierson 1994; Pierson et al. 1994) than with wind erosion. However, susceptibility to wind erosion also declines with an increase in soil organic matter (Fryrear et al. 1994) and biological crust cover (Belnap and Gillette, 1998). Both are correlated with soil stability in water.

Biological crusts consist of microorganisms (e.g. algae, cyanobacteria) and non-vascular plants (e.g. mosses and lichens) that grow on or just below the soil surface. Soil physical and chemical characteristics, along with seasonal precipitation patterns, largely determine the dominant organisms comprising the crust.

Biological crusts are important as cover and in stabilizing soil surfaces (Bond and Harris 1964, Belnap and Gardner 1993, Eldridge and Greene 1994). In some areas, depending on soil characteristics, they may increase or reduce the infiltration of water through the soil surface or enhance the retention of soil water (i.e., acting as living mulch). In general, the relative importance of biological crusts increases as annual precipitation and potential vascular plant cover decreases. If information on biological crusts is lacking in the ecological site descriptions, refer to ERAs, if available, for baseline information prior to conducting the evaluation.

Physical crusts are thin surface layers induced by the impact of raindrops on bare soil causing the soil surface to seal and absorb less water. Physical crusts are more common on silt, clay, and loam soils. When present, they are relatively thin in sandy soils. Physical and chemical crusts tend to have very low organic matter content, or contain only relatively inert organic matter that is associated with low biological activity. As this physical crust becomes more extensive, infiltration rates are reduced and overland water flow increases. Also, water can pond in flat crusted areas and will be more likely to evaporate than infiltrate into the soil.

Physical soil crusts are identified by lifting the soil surface with a pen or other sharp object and looking for cohesive layers at the soil surface which are not perforated by pores or fissures and in which there is no apparent binding by visible strands of organic material, such as cyanobacteria.

Physical crusts may exert a positive influence on reducing wind erosion (see discussion in Indicator 6, Wind Scoured, Blowouts, and/or Deposition Areas). However, their function in stabilizing the soil surface against water erosion is generally negative. Although physical crusts also include vesicular crusts, which contain numerous small air pockets or spaces similar to a sponge, these soils are still resistant to infiltration.

Chemical crusts rarely form in rangelands except on soils formed from particular parent materials (e.g., salt desert shrub communities; see the soil survey that covers the evaluation area and/or the ecological reference area) and in abandoned, irrigated agricultural fields. Where they do occur, they can reduce infiltration and increase overland water flow similar to physical crusts. They are usually identified by a white color on the soil surface.

Areas in which there is little to no soil present due to the presence of natural rock cover (nearly 100 percent surface cover by stones) or there is continuous open water (e.g., marshes in the Southeast) should be rated as "None to Slight."

9. Soil Surface Loss or Degradation

The loss or degradation of part or all of the soil surface layer or horizon is an indication of a loss in site potential (Dormaar and Willms 1998, Davenport et al. 1998). In most sites, the soil at and near the surface has the highest organic matter and nutrient content. This generally controls the maximum rate of water infiltration into the soil and is essential for successful seedling establishment (Wood et al. 1997). As erosion increases, the potential for loss of soil surface organic matter increases, resulting in further degra-dation of soil structure. Historic soil erosion may result in complete loss of this layer (Satterlund and Adams 1992, O'Hara et al. 1993). In areas with limited slope, where wind erosion does not occur, the soil may remain in place, but all characteristics that distinguish the surface from the subsurface layers are lost. Except in soils with a clearly defined horizon immediately below the surface (e.g., argillic), it is often difficult to distinguish between the loss and degradation of the soil surface. For the purposes of this indicator, this distinction is unnecessary—the objective is to determine to what extent the functional characteristics of the surface layer have been degraded. Note also that visible soil erosion is covered in discussions of Indicator 3, Pedestals and/or Terracettes, and subsurface degradation in Indicator 11, Compaction Layer.

The two primary indicators used to make this evaluation are the organic matter content (Dormaar and Willms 1998) and the structure (Karlen and Stott 1994) of the surface layer or horizon. Soil organic matter content is frequently reflected in a darker color of the soil, although high amounts of oxidized iron (common in humid climates) can obscure the organic matter. In arid soils, where organic matter contents are low, this accumulation can be quite faint. The use of a mister to wet the soil profile can help make these layers more visible.

Soil structural degradation is reflected by the loss of clearly defined structural units or aggregates at one or more scales from <1/8 inch to 3 to 4 inches. In soils with good structure, pores of various sizes are visible within the aggregates. Structural degradation is reflected in a more massive, homogeneous surface horizon and is associated with a reduction in infiltration rates (Warren et al. 1986). In heavier soils, degradation may also be reflected by more angular structural units. Comparisons to intact soil profiles at reference sites can also be used, although in cases of severe degradation, the removal of part or all of the A horizon, or of one or more textural components (e.g., Hennessey et al. 1986) may make identification of appropriate reference areas difficult.

10. Plant Community Composition and Distribution Relative to Infiltration and Runoff

Vegetation growth form is an important determinant of infiltration rate and interrill erosion (Thurow et al 1988a, b). The distribution of the amount and type of vegetation has been found to be an important factor controlling spatial and temporal variations in infiltration and interrill erosion rates on rangelands in Nevada (Blackburn 1975; Blackburn and Wood 1990), Idaho (Johnson and Gordon 1988, Blackburn and Wood 1990) and Texas (Wood and Blackburn 1984, Thurow et al. 1988a, b).

Changes in plant community composition (see Appendix 3, Functional/Structural Groups Sheet) and the distribution of species can influence (positively or negatively) the ability of a site to capture and store precipitation. Plant rooting patterns, litter production and associated decomposition processes, basal area and spatial distribution can all affect infiltration and/or runoff. In the Edwards Plateau in Texas, shifts in plant composition between bunchgrass and short grasses over time have the greatest potential to influence infiltration and soil erosion (Thurow et al. 1986, 1988a, b). An example of a composition change that reduces infiltration and increases water runoff is the conversion of desert grasslands to shrub-dominated communities (Schlesinger et al. 1990). However, infiltration and runoff are also affected when sagebrush steppe rangeland is converted to a monoculture of annual grasses. These annual grasses provide excellent watershed protection, although snow entrapment and soil water storage may be reduced by this vegetation type conversion. Care must be exercised in interpreting this indicator in different ecosystems as the same species may have different effects.

11. Compaction Layer

A compaction layer is a near-surface layer of dense soil caused by repeated impacts on or disturbances of the soil surface. Compaction can also occur below the surface at the bottom of a tillage layer. These plow pans are often found in abandoned agricultural fields. Compaction becomes a problem when it begins to limit plant growth (Wallace 1987), water infiltration (Willat and Pullar 1983, Thurow et al 1988a), or nutrient cycling processes (Hassink et al. 1993). Farm machinery, herbivore trampling (Willat and Pullar 1983, Warren et al. 1986, Chanysk and Naeth 1995), recreational and military vehicles (Webb and Wilshire 1983, Thurow et al. 1988a), foot traffic (Cole 1985), brush removal, and seeding equipment, or any other activity that repeatedly causes an impact to the soil surface can cause a compaction layer. Moist soil is more easily compacted than dry or saturated soil (Hillel 1998). Recovery processes (e.g., earthworm activity and frost heaving) are generally sufficient to limit compaction by livestock in many upland systems (e.g., Thurow et al 1988a).

A compaction layer is a structural change, not a textural change, as described in a soil survey or observed at an ecological reference area. Compacted layers in rangelands are usually less than 6 inches below the soil surface. They are detected by digging a small hole (generally less than 1-foot deep) and describing the soil structure and root morphology; this is done by a person with soils experience. These layers may be detected in some soils with the use of a penetrometer (Larson and Pierce 1993) or by simply probing the soil with a sharp rod or shovel and "feeling" for the compaction layer (Barnes et al. 1971). However, any potential compaction layer should be confirmed using multiple indicators, including direct observation of physical features. Those physical features include such things as platy or blocky, dense soil structure over less dense soil layers, horizontal root growth, and increased density (measured by weighing a known volume of oven-dry soil) (Blake and Hartge 1986). Increased resistance to a probe can be simply due to lower soil moisture or higher clay content.

12. Functional/Structural Groups

Functional/structural groups are a suite of species that are grouped together, on an ecological site basis, because of similar shoot (height and volume) or root (fibrous vs. tap) structure, photosynthetic pathways, nitrogen fixing ability, or life cycle (Chapin 1993, Dawson and Chapin 1993, Solbrig et al. 1996). Functional composition and functional diversity are the principal factors explaining plant productivity, plant percent nitrogen, plant total nitrogen, and light penetration

Table 6. Six functional/ structural groups and examples of representative species that a prairie ecological site might include.

Warm Season Tall Grasses	Big bluestem	Indiangrass
Warm Season Midgrasses	Sideoats grama	Little bluestem
Cool Season Midgrasses	Western wheatgrass	Green needlegrass
Warm Season Shortgrass	Buffalograss	Blue grama
Perennial Forbs	Dotted gayfeather	Prairie coneflower
Leguminous Shrubs	Leadplant	

(Tilman et al. 1997). The study by Tilman et al. (1997) showed that functional composition has a large impact on ecosystem processes. This and related studies have demonstrated that factors that change ecosystem composition, such as invasion by novel organisms, nitrogen deposition, disturbance frequency, fragmentation, predator decimation, species removal, and alternative management practices can have a strong effect on ecosystem processes.

The evaluator(s) should use the Functional/Structural Groups Worksheet (Appendix 3) in the development of the Reference Sheet (Appendix 2) and in the assessment of the evaluation area.

Relative dominance is based upon the relative annual production, biomass, or relative cover that each functional/structural group collectively contributes to the total. The recommended protocol to use for grouping species is composition by annual production. If the evaluator(s) doesn't have experience in estimating composition by annual production, then composition by cover may be used if appropriate reference data are available. The potential for functional/structural groups is derived by placing species into the appropriate groups from information found in the Reference Sheet that has been developed from the Functional/Structural Groups Worksheet. The list and ranking of functional/structural groups should reflect *all* of the plant (including biological crust) communities in the reference state, under the natural disturbance regime, and in the context of normal climatic variability. It should not be limited to a comparison with the historic climax community, which is the reference included in the old NRCS Range Site Descriptions. Instead, the comparison should be to communities in the reference state (in the state and transition model for the ecological site). For more information, please see the Concepts section.

The Functional/Structural Groups Worksheet can accommodate changing or adding functional group categories for different ecological sites (see Tables 6 and 7). Functional groups that are now present, but were not original components of the site (e.g., weeds, introduced plants), need to be identified on this sheet.

The number of species in each functional group is also considered when selecting the appropriate rating category on the Evaluation Sheet. If the numbers of species in many of the functional/structural plant groups have been greatly reduced, this may be an indication of loss of biotic integrity. Both the presence of functional groups and the number of species within the groups have a significant effect on ecosystem processes (Tilman et al. 1997).

Non-vascular plants (e.g., biological crusts) are included in this example since they are an important component of this Great Basin ecological site. Biological crusts are components of many ecosystems and should be included in this evaluation when appropriate.

13. Plant Mortality/Decadence

The proportion of dead or decadent (e.g., moribund, dying) to young or mature plants in the community, relative to that expected for the site under normal disturbance regimes, is an indicator of the population dynamics of the stand. If recruitment is not occurring and existing plants are either dying or dead, the integrity of the stand would be expected to decline and undesirable plants (e.g., weeds or invasives) may increase (Pyke 1995). A healthy range has a mixture of many age classes of plants relative to site potential and climatic conditions (Stoddard et al. 1975).

Only plants native to the site (or seeded plants if in a seeding) are assessed for plant mortality. Plant mortality may vary considerably depending on natural disturbance events (e.g., fire, drought, insect infestation, disease).

14. Litter Amount

Litter is any dead plant material (from both native and exotic plants) that is detached from the base of the plant. The portion of litter that is in contact with the soil surface (as opposed to standing dead vegetation) provides a source of soil organic material and raw materials for on-site nutrient cycling (Whitford 1988, 1996). All litter helps to moderate the soil microclimate and provides food for microorganisms (Hester et al. 1997). Also, the amount of litter present can play a role in enhancing the ability of the site to resist erosion. Litter helps to dissipate the energy of raindrops and overland flow, thereby reducing the potential detachment and transport of soil (Hester et al. 1997). Litter biomass represents a significant obstruction to runoff (Thurow et al. 1988a or b).

The amount of litter (herbaceous and woody) present is compared to the amount that would be expected for the same type of growing conditions in the reference state per the Reference Sheet. Litter is directly related to weather and the degree of biomass utilization each year. Therefore, climatic influences (e.g., drought, wet years) must be carefully considered in determining the rating for the amount of litter. Be careful not to confuse standing-dead plants (plant material that is not detached from the plant and is still standing) with litter during this evaluation.

Some plant communities have increased litter quantities relative to the site potential and current weather conditions. An example is the increased accumulation of litter in exotic grass communities (e.g., cheatgrass) compared to native shrub steppe plant communities. In this case, the litter in excess of the expected amount results in a downgraded rating for the site. Note in the Comments section on the Evaluation Sheet for this indicator if the litter is undergoing decomposition (darker color) or oxidation (whitish color which may also be an indication of fungal growth). In addition to amount, litter size may be important because larger litter tends to decompose more slowly and is more resistant to runoff. If litter size is considered as part of this indicator, it should be addressed in the Reference Sheet (Appendix 2).

Table 7. Selected species for nine functional/structural groups that a Great Basin Desert shrub steppe site might include.

Tall Shrubs (Deep Rooted)	Wyo. Big sagebrush		
Half Shrub	Broom Snake-weed		
Warm Season Bunchgrass	Sand Dropseed	Red Threeawn	
Cool Season Short Bunchgrass	Sandberg bluegrass		
Cool Season Mid Bunchgrass	Squirreltail	Thurbers needlegrass	Indian Ricegrass
Perennial Forbs–N Fixers	Astragalus	Lupine	
Perennial Forbs–Not N fixers	Phlox	Arrowleaf Balsamroot	Biscuitroot
Annual Grass	Cheatgrass		
Biological Crust	Moss	Lichens	

15. Annual Production

Primary production is the conversion of solar energy to chemical energy through the process of photosynthesis. Annual production, as used in this document, is the net quantity of above-ground vascular plant material produced within a year. It is an indicator of the energy captured by plants and its availability for secondary consumers in an ecosystem given current weather conditions. Production potential will change with communities or ecological sites (Whittaker 1975), biological diversity (Tilman and Downing 1994), and latitude (Cooper 1975). Annual production of the evaluation area is compared to the site potential (total annual production) as described in the Reference Sheet.

Comparisons to the Reference Sheet are based on peak above ground standing crop, no matter when the site is assessed. If utilization of vegetation has occurred or plants are in early stages of growth, the evaluator(s) is required to estimate the annual production removed or expected and include this amount when making the total site production estimate. Do not include standing dead vegetation (produced in previous years) or live tissue (woody stems) not produced in the current year as annual production.

All species (e.g., native, seeded, and weeds) alive (annual production only) in the year of the evaluation, are included in the determination of total aboveground production. Therefore, type of vegetation (e.g., native or introduced) is not an issue. For example, Rickard and Rogers (1988) found that conversion of a sagebrush steppe plant community to an exotic annual grassland greatly affected vegetation structure and function, but not above-ground biomass production.

As with the other indicators, it is important to consider all possible local and landscape level explanations for differences in production (e.g., runoff/run-on due to landscape position, weather, regional location, or different soils within an ecological site) before attributing production differences to differences in other site characteristics.

16. Invasive Plants

Invasive plants are plants that are not part of (if exotic), or are a minor component of (if native), the original plant community or communities that have the potential to become a dominant or co-dominant species on the site if their future establishment and growth is not actively controlled by management interventions. Species that become dominant for only one to several years (e.g. short-term response to drought or wildfire) are not invasive plants. This indicator deals with plants that are invasive to the evaluation area. These plants may or may not be noxious and may or may not be exotic.

Invasives can include noxious plants (i.e., plants that are listed by a State because of their unfavorable economic or ecological impacts), non-native, and native plants. Native invasive plants (e.g., pinyon pine or juniper into sagebrush steppe) must be assessed by comparing current status with potential status described in the Reference Sheet. Historical accounts, ecological reference areas, and photographs also provide information on the historical distribution of invasive native plants.

Invasive plants may impact an ecosystem's type and abundance of species, their interrelationships, and the processes by which energy and nutrients move through the ecosystem. These impacts can influence both biological organisms and physical properties of the site (Olson 1999). These impacts may range from slight to catastrophic depending on the species involved and their degree of dominance. Invasive species may adversely affect a site by increased water usage (e.g., salt cedar (tamarisk) in riparian areas) or rapid nutrient depletion (e.g., high nitrogen use by cheatgrass).

Some invasive plants (e.g., knapweeds) are capable of invading undisturbed, climax bunchgrass communities (Lacey et al. 1990), further emphasizing their use as an indicator of new ecosystem stress. Even highly diverse, species rich plant communities are susceptible to exotic species invasion (Stohlgren et al. 1999).

17. Reproductive Capability of Perennial Plants

Adequate seed production is essential to maintain populations of plants when sexual reproduction is the primary mechanism of individual plant replacement at a site. However, annual seed production of perennial plants is highly variable (Harper 1977). Since reproductive growth occurs in a modular fashion similar to the remainder of the plant (White 1979), inflorescence production (e.g., seedstalks) becomes a basic measure of reproductive potential for sexually reproducing plants, and clonal production (e.g., tillers) for vegetatively reproducing plants. Since reproductive capability of perennial plants is greatly influenced by weather, it is important to determine departure from the expected value in the Reference Sheet by evaluating management effects on this indicator. Ecological reference areas provide a good benchmark to separate weather versus management influences on this indicator.

Seed production can be assessed by comparing the number of seedstalks and/or number of seeds per seedstalk of native or seeded plants (not including invasives) in the evaluation area with what is expected as documented on the Reference Sheet. Mueggler (1975) recommended comparison of seedstalk numbers or culm length on grazed and ungrazed bluebunch wheatgrass plants as a measure of plant recruitment potential. Seed production is related to plant vigor since healthy plants are better able to produce adequate quantities of viable seed than are plants that are stressed or decadent (Hanson and Stoddart 1940).

For plants that reproduce vegetatively, the number and distribution of tillers or rhizomes is assessed relative to the expected production of these reproductive structures as documented in the Reference Sheet.

Recruitment is not assessed as a part of this indicator since plant recruitment from seed is an episodic event in many rangeland ecological sites. Therefore, evidence of recruitment (seedlings or vegetative spread) of perennial, native, or seeded plants is recorded in the comment section on the Evaluation Sheet, but is not considered in rating the reproductive capabilities of perennial plants.

This indicator considers only perennial plants. With the exception of hyperarid ecosystems (e.g., Arabian peninsula and northern Atacama desert), nearly all rangelands have the potential to support perennial plants (Whitford 2002). A plant community that lacks perennial plants is rarely, if ever, included in the reference state. Evaluation areas that have no perennial plants would be rated "Extreme to Total" for this indicator because they no longer have the capacity to (re)produce perennial plants.

18. Optional Indicators

The 17 indicators described previously represent the baseline indicators that must be assessed on all sites. Other indicators and descriptors may be developed to meet local needs. The only restriction on the development of optional indicators and their use is that they must be ecologically, not management, related. They should also significantly increase the quality of evaluation. For example, an indicator of suitability for livestock, wildlife, or special status species are not appropriate indicators to determine the health of a land unit. They may be important in the allotment or ranch evaluation, but are not included in the determination of the status of soil/site stability, hydrologic function, or biotic integrity.

Examples of two optional indicators, Biological Crusts and Vertical Vegetation Structure, are included in Table 8. Both are partially addressed by Indicator 12 (Functional/Structural Groups); however, many users find that this indicator often becomes heavily focused on plant community composition. Both optional indicators are also partially reflected by Indicator 4 (Bare Ground). Soil stabilized by visible biological crust (e.g., lichens, mosses, and algae) is not considered bare ground.

Table 8. Optional indicator and generic descriptors for biological crusts and vegetation structure.

Indicator	Extreme to Total	Moderate to Extreme	Moderate	Slight to Moderate	None to Slight
			Departure from Reference Sheet		
Biological Crusts	Found only in protected areas, very limited suite of functional groups.	Largely absent, occurring mostly in protected areas.	In protected areas and with a minor component in interspaces.	Evident throughout the site but continuity is broken.	Largely intact and nearly matches site capability.
Vertical Vegetation Structure	Number of height classes greatly reduced and/or most height classes lost and/or dramatic increase in number of height classes expected for site and/or dramatic reduction in the number or density of individuals across several height classes.	Number of height classes significantly reduced and/or more than one height class lost and/or addition of more than one height class not expected for site and/or significant reduction in the number or density of individuals across several height classes.	Number of height classes moderately reduced and/or one height class lost and/or addition of height class not expected for site and/or moderate reduction in the number or density of individuals across several height classes.	Number of height classes slightly reduced and/or slight reduction in the number or density of individuals across several height classes.	Number and type of height classes and the number and density of individuals in each height class closely match that expected for the site.

Because the Bare Ground indicator includes the spatial distribution of bare areas, it also provides some indication of the horizontal vegetation distribution.

The biological crusts indicator might be applied where these crusts play a particularly important biological or physical role (e.g., for nitrogen fixation or soil stabilization). The vegetation structure indicator is useful where variability in vertical vegetation structure within functional/structural groups affects wind erosion or the integrity of animal populations. This variability may be due to species differences within functional/structural groups, in age class distributions, or to disturbances such as fire and grazing that affect growth form.

The indicators included in these sheets are not intended to be all inclusive for all rangelands. Additional indicators may be added to the sheets to improve sensitivity in detecting changes in soil/site stability, hydrologic function, and biotic integrity.

The extensive comments received both prior to and following the publication of previous editions of this protocol included relatively few suggestions for new indicators, except where individuals wanted to include management-based indicators that are not appropriate for this protocol. There were also relatively few requests that particular indicators be dropped from the protocol, in part because users wanted to maintain consistency across evaluations. **The value of maintaining a consistent protocol often exceeds the benefit of including optional indicators**.

Step 5. Determine the Functional Status of the Three Rangeland Health Attributes (REQUIRED)
Complete the Evaluation Sheet (Appendix 1, back page).

The interpretation process is the critical link between observations of indicators and determining the degree of departure from the Reference Sheet for each health attribute in an evaluation area. The interpretation of the indicators and the selection of the degree of departure of the rangeland health attributes (soil/site stability, hydrologic function, and biotic integrity) are made at the bottom of Page 2 of the Evaluation Sheet. This summary rating is made by reviewing the indicator ratings and comments from all of the sheets, to arrive at a single degree of departure from the Reference Sheet for each attribute.

A "preponderance of evidence" approach is used to select the appropriate departure category for each attribute. This decision is based, in part, on where the majority of the indicators for each attribute fall under the five categories. For example, if four of the soil/site stability indicators are in the "moderate" and six are in the "slight to moderate" departure from the ecological site description/ERA categories, the soil/site stability attribute departure would be rated as "slight to moderate" assuming that the evaluator(s) interpretation of other information and local ecological knowledge supported this rating. However, if one of the four indicators in the "moderate" category is particularly important for the site (e.g., bare ground), a rating of "moderate" can be supported.

Once an evaluation is made for each attribute, managers may use the attribute evaluation to identify where more information (monitoring and/or inventory data) is required. This information should be reviewed if available, or if not available, the information should be collected. Therefore, these areas (i.e., moderate departure) are often ideal for the implementation of monitoring studies since they should be the most responsive to management activities. However, additional monitoring may be useful regardless of the departure rating, dependent upon future changes in uses or management of an area.

This procedure relies upon the collective experience and knowledge of the evaluator(s) to classify each indicator and then to interpret the collective rating for the indicators into one summary rating of departure for each attribute. The rating of each indicator and the interpretation into a collective rating for each attribute is not apprentice-level work. This procedure has been developed for use by experienced, knowledgeable evaluator(s). It is not intended that this assessment procedure be used by new and/or inexperienced employees, without training and assistance by more experienced and knowledgeable employees.

Applications to Larger Areas

Although the procedure described in this document is based upon a site-specific evaluation area, it can be applied at a watershed, pasture, allotment, or ranch level with the proper study design. Tools to help apply this to larger areas include topographic maps, water locations, grazing-use pattern maps, inventory or monitoring information, soil surveys, geographical information system (GIS) technology, and local knowledge. Individual site evaluations are made on selected rangeland ecological sites. Areas in the same rangeland ecological site, with the same ratings for the three rangeland health attributes, may be mapped and consolidated within a pasture or management unit (e.g., ranch or allotment). Where ecological site units are too small to be mapped, a "complex" map unit can be applied. Each complex includes two or more ecological sites. The attribute ratings for each ecological site in a complex are included in the map legend "ecological sites."

Additional studies or information may be required to confirm these ratings. The protocol described in this document is not intended to be used as a "stand-alone" tool to determine the final "health" or functional status of the three attributes of rangeland health.

Attribute ratings may stimulate further actions (e.g., review or initiation of inventory, monitoring, or different assessments; communication with various groups interested in the management of the area) to determine the reason for these ratings or determine if the trend is satisfactory under existing management. Areas in which one or more attributes is rated "Extreme to Total" or "Moderate to Extreme" usually have easily identified severe resource problems and have often crossed an ecological threshold. The cost effectiveness of management actions in these areas is often lower than in areas that have not yet crossed a threshold. Changes in management are not appropriate based solely on the evaluation of range health per the procedures in this document.

Summary

Qualitative assessments of rangeland health provide land managers and technical assistance specialists with a good communication tool for use with the public. This technique, in association with quantitative monitoring and inventory information (e.g., Table 2 in Concepts section), can be used to provide early warnings of resource problems. This procedure does not establish the cause of rangeland health problems; it simply identifies where a problem exists. This procedure is not intended nor designed to replace quantitative monitoring, serve as a trend study, or provide data that can be aggregated for a national report on rangeland health.

However, more research is needed to quantify indicator attributes and identify thresholds for rangeland health. Once this information is available, the assessment of rangeland health will become more quantitative and less reliant on qualitative assessment of the indicators. This document will continue to be revised as a result of continued research and application of this procedure. Where possible, ecological site-specific indicators and descriptors will be developed. The interpretation of the indicators will continue to evolve as our understanding of ecological dynamics (e.g., as described in state and transition diagrams) continues to grow. As the concept of rangeland health continues to evolve and mature, the application of this concept and protocol will also evolve.

Literature Cited

Anderson, E.W. 1974. Indicators of soil movement on range watersheds. Journal of Range Management 27:244–247.

Barnes, K.K., W.M. Carleton, H.M. Taylor, R.I. Throckmorton, and G.E. Vanden Berg (organizers). 1971. Compaction of agricultural soils. American Society of Agricultural Engineers. St. Joseph, Michigan.

Belnap, J. and J. S. Gardner. 1993. Soil microstructure in soil of the Colorado Plateau: The role of the cyanobacterium *Microcoleus vaginatus*. Great Basin Naturalist 53: 40–47.

Belnap, J. and D.A. Gillette. 1998. Vulnerability of desert biological crusts to wind erosion: the influences of crust development, soil texture and disturbance. Journal of Arid Environments 39:133–42.

Benkobi, L., M.J. Trlica, and J.L. Smith. 1993. Soil loss as affected by different combinations of surface litter and rock. Journal of Environmental Quality 22:657–61.

Bestelmeyer, B.T., J.R. Brown, K.M. Havstad, R. Alexander, G. Chavez, and J.E. Herrick. 2002. Viewpoint: issues in the development and use of state and transition models for rangeland management. Journal of Range Management 56:114–126.

Bestelmeyer, B.T., J.E. Herrick, J.R. Brown, D.A. Trujillo, and K.M. Havstad. 2004. Land management in the American Southwest: approaching ecosystem complexity with conceptual state-and-transition models. Environmental Management. 34:38–51.

Blackburn, W.H. 1975. Factors influencing infiltration and sediment production of semiarid rangelands. Nevada Water Resources Res. 11:929–937.

Blackburn, W.H. and M.K. Wood. 1990. Influence of soil frost on infiltration of shrub coppice dune and dune interspace soils in southern Nevada. Great Basin Naturalist. 50:41–46.

Blackburn, W.H. and F.B. Pierson Jr. 1994. Sources of variation in interrill erosion on rangelands. *In* W.H. Blackburn, F.B. Pierson Jr., G.E. Schuman, and R. Zartman (eds). Variability in rangeland water erosion processes, Pages 1-10. Madison, Wisconsin: Soil Science Society of America.

Blackburn, W.H., F.B. Pierson, C.L. Hanson, T.L. Thurow, and A.L. Hanson. 1992. The spatial and temporal influences of vegetation on surface soil factors in semiarid rangelands. Transactions of the ASAE 35:479–486.

Blake, G.R. and K.H. Hartge. 1986. Bulk density. *In* A. Klute (ed). Methods of soil analysis. Part I. Second Edition, Pages 363-75. Agron. Monogr. 9. Madison, Wisconsin: ASA and SSSA.

Bond, R.D. and J.R. Harris. 1964. The influence of the mircoflora on the physical properties of soils. I. Effects associated with filamentous algae and fungi. Australian Journal of Soil Research 2:111–122.

Borman, M.M. and D.A. Pyke. 1994. Successional theory and the desired plant community approach. Rangelands 16:82–85.

Bryan, R.B. 1987. Processes and significance of rill development. Pages 1-16 *In* Bryan, R.B. (ed.), Rill erosion: processes and significance. Catena Supplement, 8, Catena Verlag, Germany.

Cerda, A. 1999. Parent material and vegetation affect soil erosion in eastern Spain. Soil Science Society of America Journal 63:362–68.

Chanasyk, D.S. and M.A. Naeth. 1995. Grazing impacts on bulk density and soil strength in the foothills fescue grasslands of Alberta, Canada. Canadian Journal of Soil Science.

Chapin, F.S., III. 1993. Functional role of growth forms in ecosystem and global processes. Pages 287-312 IN: Ehleringer, J.R. and Field, C.B. (eds.), Scaling physiological processes: leaf to globe. Academic Press, San Diego, California.

Chepil, W.S. 1945. Dynamics of wind erosion IV. The translocating and abrasive action of the wind. Soil Science 61:167–171.

Chepil, W.S. and N.P Woodruff. 1963. The physics of wind erosion and its control. Advances in Agronomy 15:211–302.

Cole, D.N. 1985. Recreational trampling effects on six habitat types in western Montana. Research Paper INT-350. USDA-USFS Intermountain Research Station: Ogden, Utah.

Cooper, J.P. (ed.) 1975. Photosynthesis and productivity in different environments. Cambridge University Press, Cambridge, Massachusetts.

Davenport, D.W., D.D. Breshears, B.P. Wilcox, and C.D. Allen. 1998. Viewpoint: sustainability of piñon-juniper ecosystems—a unifying perspective of soil erosion thresholds. Journal of Range Management 51:231–240.

Daubenmire, R. 1968. Plant communities: a textbook of plant Synecology. Harper & Row, New York, New York.

Dawson, T.E. and F.S. Chapin, III. 1993. Grouping plants by their form-function characteristics as an avenue for simplification in scaling between leaves. Pages 313-322, In: Ehleringer, J.R. and Field, C.B. (eds.), Scaling physiological processes: leaf to globe. Academic Press, San Diego, California.

Dormar, J.F. and W.D. Willms. 1998. Effect of forty-four years of grazing on fescue grassland soils. Journal of Range Management 51:122–26.

Eldridge, D.J. and S.B. Greene. 1994. Microbiotic soil crusts: a review of their roles in soil and ecological processes in rangelands of Australia. Australian Journal of Soil Research 32:389–415.

Elzinga, C.L., D.W. Salzer, and J.W. Willoughby. 1998. Measuring and monitoring plant populations, Technical Reference 1730-1. 477pp. (Available online at http://www.blm.gov/nstc/library/techref.htm).

Fryrear, D.W., C.A. Krammes, D.L. Williamson, and T.M. Zobeck. 1994. Computing the wind erodible fraction of soils. Journal of Soil and Water Conservation 49:183–88.

Gibbens, R.P., J.M. Tromble, J.T. Hennessy, and M. Cardenas. 1983. Soil movement in mesquite duneland and former grasslands of southern New Mexico from 1933 to 1980. Journal of Range Management 36:145–148.

Gillette, D.A. and T.R. Walker. 1977. Characteristics of airborne particles produced by wind erosion of sandy soil, High Plains of West Texas. Soil Science 123:97–110.

Gillette, D.A., I.H. Blifford, Jr., and D.W. Fryrear. 1974. The influence of wind velocity on the size distributions of aerosols generated by the wind erosion of soils. Journal of Geophysical Research 79:4068–4075.

Gillette, D.A., I.H. Blifford, Jr., and I.H. Fenster. 1972. Measurements of aerosol-size distribution and vertical fluxes of aerosols on land subject to wind erosion. Journal of Applied Meteorology 11:977–987.

Goff, B.F., G.C. Bent, and G.E. Hart. 1993. Erosion response of a disturbed sagebrush steppe hillslope. Journal of Environmental Quality 22:698–709.

Gould, W.L. 1982. Wind erosion curtailed by shrub control. Journal of Range Management 35:563–66.

Gutierrez, J. and I. I. Hernandez. 1996. Runoff and interrill erosion as affected by grass cover in a semi-arid rangeland of northern Mexico. Journal of Arid Environments 34:287–295.

Hagen, L.J. 1984. Soil aggregate abrasion by impacting sand and soil particles. Transactions of the American Society of Agricultural Engineering 27:805–808.

Hansen, W.R. and L.A. Stoddart. 1940. Effects of grazing upon bunch wheatgrass. Amer. Soc. Agron. J. 32:278–289.

Harper, J.L. 1977. Population biology of plants. Academic Press, New York.

Hassink, J., L.A. Bouwman, K.B. Zwart, and L. Brussaard. 1993. Relationships between habitable pore space, soil biota, and mineralization rates in grassland soils. Soil Biology and Biochemistry 25:47–55.

Heady, H.F. and R.D. Child. 1994. Rangeland ecology and management. Westview Press, San Francisco, California.

Hennessy, J.T., B. Kies, R.P. Gibbens, and J.M. Tromble. 1986. Soil sorting by forty-five years of wind erosion on a southern New Mexico range. Soil Science Society of America Journal 50:391–394.

Hennessy, J.T., R.P. Gibbens, J.M. Tromble, and M. Cardenas. 1983. Vegetation changes from 1935 to 1980 in mesquite dunelands and former grasslands of southern New Mexico. Journal of Range Management 36:370–374.

Herrick, J.E., J.W. Van Zee, K.M. Havstad, and W.G. Whitford. 2005. Monitoring manual for grassland, shrubland and savanna ecosystems. USDA-ARS Jornada Experimental Range, Las Cruces, New Mexico.

Herrick, J.E., W.G. Whitford, A.G. de Soyza, J.W. Van Zee, K.M. Havstad, C.A. Seybold, and M. Walton. 2001. Soil aggregate stability kit for field-based soil quality and rangeland health evaluations. CATENA 44:27–35.

Hester, J.W., T.L. Thurow, and C.A. Taylor Jr., 1997. Hydrologic characteristics of vegetation types as affected by prescribed burning. Journal of Range Management 50:199–204.

Hillel, D. 1998. Environmental soil physics. San Diego: Academic Press.

Hudson, N. 1993. Field measurement of soil erosion and runoff. Food and Agriculture Organization of the United Nations (FAO), Rome.

Johnson, C.W. and N.E. Gordon. 1988. Runoff and erosion from rainfall simulator plots on sagebrush rangelands. Transactions of the ASAE. 31(2):421–427.

Karlen, D.L. and D.E. Stott. 1994. A framework for evaluating physical and chemical indicators of soil quality. *In* J.W. Doran, D.C. Coleman, D.F. Bezdicek, and B.A. Stewart (eds). Defining soil quality for a sustainable environment, SSSA Special Publication Number 35. Pages 53-72. Soil Science Society of America.

Karr, J. R. 1992. Ecological integrity: Protecting earth's life support systems. p. 223-238. *In* R. Costanza, B. G. Norton, and B. D. Haskell (eds.), Ecosystem health—new goals for environmental management, Island Press, Washington, DC.

Lacey J., P. Husby, and G. Handle. 1990. Observations on spotted and diffuse knapweek invasion into ungrazed bunchgrass communities in western Montana. Rangelands 12:30–32.

Lackey, R. T. 1998. Ecosystem management: paradigms and prattle, people and prizes. Renewable Resources Journal 16:8–13.

Larson, W.E. and F.J. Pierce. 1993. The dynamics of soil quality as a measure of sustainable management. *In* J.W. Doran, D.C. Coleman, D.F. Bezdicek, and B.A. Stewart (eds). Defining soil quality for a sustainable environment, SSSA Special Publication Number 35. Pages 27-51.

Martin, S.C. and H.L. Morton. 1993. Mesquite control increases grass density and reduces soil loss in southern Arizona. Journal of Range Management 46:170–175.

Morgan, R.P.C. 1986. Soil erosion and conservation. Davidson, D.A. (ed.), Longman Scientific and Technical, Wiley, New York.

Morgan, R.P.C., K. McIntyre, A.W. Vickers, J.N. Quinton, and R.J. Rickson. 1997. A rainfall simulation study of soil erosion on rangeland in Swaziland. Soil Technology 11:291–99.

Morin, J. and J. Van Winkel. 1996. The effect of raindrop impact and sheet erosion on infiltration rate and crust formation. Soil Science Society of America Journal 60:1223–1227.

Mueggler, W.F. 1975. Rate and pattern of vigor recovery in Idaho fescue and bulebunch wheatgrass. Journal of Range Management 28:198–204.

National Research Council. 1994. Rangeland health: new methods to classify, inventory, and monitor rangelands. National Academy Press, Washington, DC. National Research Council. 180p.

NRCS Soil Quality Institute, NRCS Grazing Lands Technology Institute, NRCS National Soil Survey Center, USDA-ARS Jornada Experimental Range, USDI Bureau of Land Management. 2002. Rangeland soil quality information sheets (http://soils.usda.gov/sqi/sqiproductlist.html).

O'Hara, S.L., F.A. Street, and T.P. Burt. 1993. Accelerated soil erosion around a Mexican highland lake caused by pre-hispanic agriculture. Nature 362:48–51.

Olson, B.E. 1999. Impacts of noxious weeds on ecological and economic systems. Pages 4-18, *In* Sheley, R.L. and Petroff, J.K. (ed.), Biology and management of noxious rangeland weeds. Oregon State University Press, Corvallis, Oregon.

Pellant, M. 1996. Use of indicators to qualitatively assess rangeland health. *Rangelands in a Sustainable Biosphere*. (Ed. N.E. West), pp 434-435. Proc. Vth International Rangeland Congress. Society for Range Management. Denver, Colorado.

Pierson, F.B., W. H. Blackburn, S.S. Van Vactor, and J.C. Wood. 1994. Partitioning small scale spatial variability of runoff and erosion on sagebrush rangeland. Water Resources Bulletin 30:1081–1089.

Pierson, F.B., K.E. Spaeth, M.A. Weltz, and D.H. Carlson. 2002. Hydrologic response of diverse western rangelands. Journal of Range Management 55:558–570.

Pimm, S.L. 1984. The complexity and stability of ecosystems. Nature. 307:321–326.

Puigdefábregas, J. and G. Sánchez. 1996. Geomorphological implications of vegetation patchiness on semi-arid slopes. *In* Anderson, M.G., and S.M. Brooks. Advances in Hillslope Processes. Pages 1029-1060. Vol. 2. London: John Wiley & Sons Ltd.

Pye, K. 1987. Aeolian dust and dust deposits. Academic Press. San Diego, California.

Pyke, D.A. 1995. Population diversity with special reference to rangeland plants. Pages 21-32, *In* West, N.E. (ed.), Biodiversity of rangelands. Natural Resources and Environmental Issues, Vol. IV, College of Natural Resources, Utah State University, Logan.

Pyke, D.A., J.E. Herrick, P. Shaver, and M. Pellant. 2002. Rangeland health attributes and indicators for qualitative assessment. Journal of Range Management 55:584–297.

Quansah, C. 1985. The effect of soil type, slope, flow rate and their interactions on detachment by overland flow with and without rain. Pages 19-28 *In* Jungerius, P.D. (ed.), Soils and geomorphology. Catena Supplement, 6, Catena Verlag, Germany.

Rapport, D.J. 1995. Ecosystem health: exploring the territory. Ecosystem Health 1:5–13.

Rapport, D.J., C. Gaudet, J.R. Karr, J.S. Baron, C. Bohlen, W Jackson, B. Jones, R.J. Naiman, B. Norton, and M.M. Pollock. 1998. Evaluating landscape health: integrating societal goals and biophysical process. Journal of Environmental Management 53:1–15.

Rasmussen, G.A., M. Pellant, and D. Pyke. 1999. Reliability of a qualitative assessment process on rangeland ecosystems. People and rangelands, building the future. (Eds. D. Eldridge and D. Freudenberger), pp 781-782. Proc. VIth International Rangeland Congress. 1999 VI International Rangeland Congress, Inc.

Rickard, W.H. and L.E. Rogers. 1988. Plant community characteristics and responses. Pages 109-179. *In* Rickard, W.H., L.E. Rogers, B.E. Vaughn, and S.F. Liebetrau (eds). Shrub-steppe: balance and change in a semiarid terrestrial ecosystems. Developments in agricultural and managed-forest ecology, Elsevier, New York.

Satterlund, D.R. and P.W. Adams. 1992. Wildland Watershed Management, 2nd ed. New York: John Wiley & Sons, Inc.

Schlesinger, W.H., J.F. Reynolds, G.L. Cunningham, L.F. Huenneke, W.M. Jarrell, R.A. Virginia, and W.G. Whitford. 1990. Biological feedbacks in global desertification. Science 247:1043–1048.

Seybold, C.A., J.E. Herrick, and J.J. Brejda. 1999. Soil resilience: a fundamental component of soil quality. Soil Science 164:224–234.

Sheley, R.L., J.K. Petroff, and M.M. Borman. 1999. Introduction. *In* R.L. Sheley and J.K. Petroff (eds). Biology and management of noxious rangeland weeds. Pages 1-3. Oregon State University Press, Corvallis, Oregon.

Smith, D.D. and W.H. Wischmeier. 1962. Rainfall erosion. Advances in Agronomy 14:109-148.

Smith, E. L. 1999. The myth of range/watershed health. Pp. 6-11, *In* Riparian and watershed management in the interior northwest: an interdisciplinary perspective. Oregon State University Extension Service Special Report 1001, Corvallis, Oregon.

Society for Range Management. 1999. A glossary of terms used in range management. Society for Range Management. Denver, Colorado. 20p.

Soil Science Society of America. 1997. Glossary of soil science terms. Soil Science Society of America. Madison, Wisconsin. 138p.

Solbrig, O.T., E. Medina, and J.F. Silva. 1996. Biodiversity and savanna ecosystem processes: a global perspective. Springer, New York.

Spaeth, K.E., M.A. Weltz, H.D. Fox, and F.B. Pierson. 1994. Spatial pattern analysis of sagebrush vegetation and potential influences on hydrology and erosion. *In* W.H. Blackburn, F.B. Pierson Jr., G.E. Schuman, and R. Zartman (eds). Variability in rangeland water erosion processes. Pages 35-50. Madison, Wisconsin: Soil Science Society of America.

Stoddard, L.A., A.D. Smith, and T.W. Box. 1975. Range management. McGraw-Hill Book Company.

Stohlgren, T.J., D. Binkley, G.W. Chong, M.A. Kalkhan, L.D. Schell, K.A. Bull, Y. Otsuki, G. Newman, M. Bashkin, and Y. Son. 1999. Exotic plant species invade hot spots of native plant diversity. Ecological Monograph 69:25–46.

Stringham, T. K., W. C. Krueger, and P. L. Shaver. 2001. States, transitions and thresholds: Further refinement for rangeland applications. Corvallis, Oregon, Oregon State University Agricultural Experiment Station.

Task Group on Unity in Concepts and Terminology. 1995. New concepts for assessment of rangeland condition. Journal of Range Management 48:271–282.

Thurow, T.L., W.H. Blackburn, and C.A. Taylor, Jr. 1986. Hydrologic characteristics of vegetation types as affected by livestock grazing systems, Edwards Plateau, Texas. Journal of Range Management 39:505–509.

Thurow, T.L., W.H. Blackburn, and C.A. Taylor, Jr. 1988a. Infiltration and interrill erosion responses to selected livestock grazing strategies, Edwards Plateau, Texas. Journal of Range Management 41:296–302.

Thurow, T.L., W.H. Blackburn, and C.A. Taylor, Jr. 1988b. Some vegetation responses to selected livestock grazing strategies, Edwards Plateau, Texas. Journal of Range Management 41:108–114.

Tilman, D. and J.A. Downing. 1994. Biodiversity and stability in grasslands. Nature. 367:363–367.

Tilman, D., J. Knops, D. Wedin, P. Reich, M. Ritchie, and E. Siemann 1997. The influence of functional diversity and composition on ecosystem processes. Science Vol. 277:1300–1302.

Tiscareño-Lopez, M., V.L. Lopes, J.J. Stone and L.J. Lane. 1993. Sensitivity analysis of the WEPP watershed model for rangeland applications. 1. Hillslope Processes. Transactions of the ASAE 36:1659–72.

Tongway, D. J. 1994. Rangeland soil condition assessment manual. CSIRO Publishing, Melbourne, Australia.

U.S. Department of Agriculture, Natural Resources Conservation Service. 1997. National range and pasture handbook. Washington, DC. U.S. Department of Agriculture.

U.S. Department of the Interior, Bureau of Land Management. 1973. Determination of erosion condition class, Form 7310-12. Washington, DC.

U.S. Department of the Interior, Bureau of Land Management. 1993. Riparian area management: process for assessing proper functioning condition. Technical Reference 1737-9. Service Center, Denver, Colorado.

Vallentine, J.F. 1990. Grazing management. Academic Press, Berkeley, California.

Wagner, R.E. 1989. History and development of site and condition criteria in the Bureau of Land Management. p. 35-48. *In* W.K. Lauenroth and W.A. Laycock (eds.), Secondary succession and the evaluation of rangeland condition, Westview, Boulder, Colorado.

Wallace, L.L. 1987. Effects of clipping and soil compaction on growth, morphology and mycorrhizal colonization of *Schizachyrium scoparium* a C4 bunchgrass. Oecologia 72:423–428.

Warren, S.D., T.L. Thurow, W.H. Blackburn, and N.E. Garza. 1986. The influence of livestock trampling under intensive rotation grazing on soil hydrologic characteristics. Journal of Range Management 39:491–95.

Webb, R.H. and H.G. Wilshire. 1983. Environmental effects of off-road vehicles: Impacts and management in arid regions. New York: Springer-Verlag.

Weltz, M.A., M.R. Kidwell, and H.D. Fox. 1998. Influence of abiotic and biotic factors in measuring and modeling soil erosion on rangelands: state of knowledge. Journal of Range Management 51:482–95.

West, N.E., K. McDaniel, E.L. Smith, P.T. Tuellerand, and S. Leonard. 1994. Monitoring and interpreting ecological integrity on arid and semi-arid lands of the western United States. Report 37. New Mexico State University, New Mexico Range Improvement Task Force.

White, J. 1979. The plant as a metapopulation. Annual Review of Ecology and Systematics 10:109–145.

Whitford, W.G. 1988. Decomposition and nutrient cycling in disturbed arid ecosystems. Pages 136-161, *In* Allen, E.B. (ed.) The reconstruction of disturbed arid lands. American Association for the Advancement of Science, Westview Press, Boulder, Colorado.

Whitford, W.G. 1996. The importance of the biodiversity of soil biota in arid ecosystems. Biodiversity and Conservation 5:185–195.

Whitford, W. G. 2002. Ecology of Desert Systems. San Diego: Academic Press.

Whittaker, R.H. 1975. Communities and ecosystems, 2nd edition. Macmillan, New York.

Wicklum, D. and R. W. Davies. 1995. Ecosystem health and integrity. Canadian Journal of Botany 73:997–1000.

Willat, S.T. and D.M. Pullar. 1983. Changes in soil physical properties under grazed pastures. Australian Journal of Soil Research 22:343–348.

Wood, M.K. and W.H. Blackburn. 1984. Vegetation and soil responses to cattle grazing systems in the Texas Rolling Plains. Journal of Range Management. 37:303–308.

Wood, M.K. E. Eckert Jr., W.H. Blackburn, and F.F. Peterson. 1997. Influence of crusting soil surfaces on emergence and establishment of crested wheatgrass, squirreltail, Thurber needlegrass and fourwing saltbush. Journal of Range Management 35:282–87.

Glossary

Abundance: The total number of individuals of a species in an area, population, or community (SRM 1999).

Accelerated erosion: Erosion in excess of natural rates, usually as a result of anthropogenic activities (SSSA 1997).

Age classes: The distribution of different ages of the same species or group of species on a site.

Annual plant: A plant that completes its life cycle and dies in 1 year or less (SRM 1999).

Annual production: The net quantity of aboveground vascular plant material produced within a year. *Synonym:* net aboveground primary production.

Assessment: The process of estimating or judging the value or functional status of ecological processes (e.g., rangeland health) in a location at a moment in time.

At risk: Rangelands that have a reversible loss in productive capability and increased vulnerability to irreversible degradation based upon an evaluation of current conditions of the soil and ecological processes (NRC 1994). At risk designation may point out the need for additional information needed to better quantify the functional status of an attribute.

Attribute: One of the three components, soil/site stability, hydrologic function, and biotic integrity that collectively define rangeland health.

Badland: A land type consisting of steep or very steep barren land, usually broken by an intricate maze of narrow ravines, sharp crests, and pinnacles resulting from serious erosion of soft geologic materials (SRM 1999).

Bare ground (bare soil): All land surface not covered by vegetation, rock, or litter (SRM 1999). As used in this document, visible biological crusts and standing dead vegetation are included in cover estimates or measurements and therefore are **not** bare ground (e.g., mineral soil).

Basal area (plants): The cross-sectional area of the stem or stems of a plant or of all plants in a stand. Herbaceous and small woody plants are measured at or near the ground level; larger woody plants are measured at breast or other designated height. *Synonym:* basal cover (SRM 1999).

Basal cover (plants): The percent of soil surface covered by plant bases. *Synonym:* basal area (SRM 1999).

Biological crust: Microorganisms (e.g., lichens, algae, cyanobacteria, microfungi) and non-vascular plants (e.g., mosses, lichens) that grow on or just below the soil surface. *Synonym:* microbiotic crust and cryptogamic crust.

Biomass (plants): The total amount of living plants above and below ground in an area at a given time (SRM 1999). As used in this document, biomass refers only to parts of standing living plants above ground, and not the roots.

Biotic integrity: Capacity of a site to support characteristic functional and structural communities in the context of normal variability, to resist loss of this function and structure due to a disturbance, and to recover following such disturbance. (One of the three attributes of rangeland health.)

Blowout: An excavation in areas of loose soil, usually sand, produced by wind; a breakthrough or rupture of a soil surface attributable to hydraulic pressure, usually associated with sand boils (SRM 1999).

Bunch grass: A grass having the characteristic growth habit of forming a bunch; lacking stolons or rhizomes (SRM 1999).

Canopy Cover: The percentage of the ground covered by a vertical projection of the outermost perimeter of the natural spread of foliage of plants. Small openings within the canopy are included. *Synonym:* crown cover (USDA 1997).

Chemical soil crust: A soil-surface layer, ranging in thickness from a few millimeters to a few centimeters, that is formed when chemical compounds become concentrated on the soil surface. They can reduce infiltration and increase overland water flow similar to physical crusts. They are usually identified by a white color on the soil surface.

Climate: The average or prevailing weather conditions of a place over a period of years (SRM 1999).

Climax plant community (climax): The final or stable biotic community in a successional series; it is self-perpetuating and in equilibrium with the physical habitat (SRM 1999).

Community pathway: Shifts in plant species compositions among biological communities within a single state.

Compaction layer: A near surface layer of dense soil caused by the repeated impact on or disturbance of the soil surface. When soil is compacted, soil grains are rearranged to decrease the void space and bring them into closer contact with one another, thereby increasing the bulk density (SSSA 1997).

Composition: The proportions of various plant species in relation to the total on a given area; it may be expressed in terms of cover, density, weight, etc. *Synonym:* Species composition (SRM 1999).

Cool-season plant: A plant which generally makes the major portion of its growth during the late fall, winter, and early spring. Cool season grasses generally exhibit the C-3 photosynthetic pathway. cf. warm-season plants (SRM 1999).

Cover: Percentage of material, other than bare ground, covering the land surface. It may include live and standing dead vegetation, litter, biological crust, cobble, gravel, stones, and bedrock. Ground cover plus bare ground would total 100 percent. *Synonym:* ground cover.

Decomposition: The biochemical breakdown of organic matter into its original compounds and nutrients.

Deposition area: An area offsite from where the original soil erosion occurred that now has the soil deposits from the original soil erosion area.

Descriptor: The narrative that describes the indicator characteristics under each of the five rating categories (Extreme to Total, Moderate to Extreme, Moderate, Slight to Moderate, and None to Slight) in the Rangeland Health Indicator Evaluation Matrix. The "default descriptor" is printed in the Matrix, while the "revised descriptor" is completed by the evaluators if the default descriptor does not fit the characteristics of a particular indicator for a particular ecological site.

Desired plant community: Of the several plant communities that may occupy a site, the one that has been identified through a management plan to best meet the plan's objectives for the site. It must protect the site as a minimum (SRM 1999).

Dominant species: Plant species or species groups, which by means of their number, coverage, or size, have considerable influence or control upon the conditions of existence of associated species (SRM 1999). Daubenmire (1968) defines dominant species as "those species whose removal would bring about the greatest readjustments in the edaphic, aerial, and biotic character of their ecosystem. They are often the tallest plants" and "where there is little difference in size, dominance is determined primarily by numbers of individuals." For purposes of this document, *Interpreting Indicators of Rangeland Health*, dominant plants are those of the greatest size per unit area as measured by biomass, production, or cover.

Ecological processes: Ecological processes include the water cycle (the capture, storage, and redistribution of precipitation), energy flow (conversion of sunlight to plant and animal matter), and nutrient cycle (the cycle of nutrients such as nitrogen and phosphorus through the physical and biotic components of the environment). Ecological processes functioning within a normal range of variation will support specific plant and animal communities.

Ecological reference area: An area representing a single ecological site in which ecological processes are functioning within a normal range of variability and the plant community has adequate resistance to and resistance from most disturbances. These areas do not need to be pristine, historically unused lands (e.g., climax plant communities or relict areas).

Ecological site: A kind of land with specific physical characteristics which differs from other kinds of land in its ability to produce distinctive kinds and amounts of vegetation and in its response to management. Apparently synonymous with ecological type used by USDA Forest Service. Synonym: Rangeland Ecological Site (SRM 1999).

Ecological site description: Description of the soils, uses, and potential of a kind of land with specific physical characteristics to produce distinctive kinds and amounts of vegetation.

Ecosystem: Organisms together with their abiotic environment, forming an interacting system, inhabiting an identifiable space (SRM 1999).

Energy flow: Conversion of sunlight to plant and animal matter; one of the ecological processes.

Erosion: Detachment and movement of soil or rock fragments by water, wind, ice, gravity; the land surface worn away by running water, wind, ice, or other geological agents, including such processes as gravitational creep (SRM 1999).

Evaluation area: The area (generally 1/2 to 1 acre in size) where the evaluation of rangeland health attributes takes place.

Evaluator(s): The person or persons conducting the evaluation of rangeland health on an evaluation area.

Exclosure: An area fenced to exclude animals (SRM 1999).

Exotic plant: A plant growing on or occurring in an ecosystem beyond its natural range of existence or natural zone of potential dispersal.

Flow pattern: The path that water takes (i.e., accumulates) as it moves across the soil surface during overland flow.

Foliar Cover: The percentage of ground covered by the vertical projection of the aerial portion of plants. Small openings in the canopy and intraspecific overlap are excluded. Foliar cover is always less than canopy cover; either may exceed 100 percent (USDA 1997).

Forb: Any broad-leafed, herbaceous plant other than those in the Poaceae, Cyperaceae, and Juncaceae families (SRM 1999).

Functional/structural groups: A suite or group of species that because of similar shoot or root structure, photosynthetic pathways, nitrogen fixing ability, life cycle, etc., are grouped together on an ecological site basis.

Functioning: (1) Refers to the rangeland health attributes where the majority (see definition of "preponderance of evidence") of the associated indicators are rated as having little or no deviation from that described in the Reference Sheet (Appendix 2) for the ecological site; (2) Refers to the presence and integrity of ecological processes (energy flow, water cycling, and nutrient cycling) being within the range of expectations for the ecological site.

Geomorphology: The science that studies the evolution of the earth's surface. The science of landforms (SSSA 1997).

Grass: Members of the plant family Poaceae (SRM 1999).

Ground cover: Percentage of material, other than bare ground, covering the land surface. It may include live and standing dead vegetation, litter, biological crust, cobble, gravel, stones, and bedrock. Ground cover plus bare ground would total 100 percent.

Ground cover (as used in this document): Percentage of material, other than bare ground, covering the land surface. It may include live and standing dead vegetation, *biological soil crusts*, litter, cobble, gravel, stones, and bedrock. Ground cover plus bare ground would total 100 percent.

Gully: A furrow, channel, or miniature valley, usually with steep sides through which water commonly flows during and immediately after rains or snowmelt (SRM 1999). Small channels eroded by concentrated water flow.

Headcut: Abrupt elevation drops in the channel of a gully that accelerate erosion as it undercuts the gully floor and migrates upstream.

Half-shrub: A perennial plant with a woody base whose annually produced stems die each year (SRM 1999).

Healthy rangelands: The degree to which the integrity of the soil, vegetation, water, and air, as well as the ecological processes of the rangeland ecosystem, are balanced and sustained. Integrity is defined as maintenance of the structure and functional attributes characteristic of a locale, including normal variability (SRM 1999). *Synonym:* rangeland health.

Historic climax plant community: The plant community that was best adapted to the unique combination of factors associated with the ecological site. It was in a natural dynamic equilibrium with the historic biotic, abiotic, climatic factors on its ecological site in North America at the time of European immigration and settlement (USDA 1997).

Hydrologic function: The capacity of the site to capture, store, and safely release water from rainfall, run-on, and snowmelt (where relevant), to resist a reduction in this capacity, and to recover this capacity following degradation (one of the three attributes of rangeland health).

Increaser: For a given plant community, those species that increase in amount as a result of a specific abiotic/biotic influence or management practice (SRM 1999).

Indicator: Components of a system whose characteristics (e.g., presence or absence, quantity, distribution) are used as an index of an attribute (e.g., rangeland health) that are too difficult, inconvenient, or expensive to measure.

Infiltration: The entry of water into the soil (SSSA 1997).

Interrill erosion: The removal of a fairly uniform layer of soil on a multitude of relatively small areas by splash due to raindrop impact and by sheet flow (SSSA 1997).

Invader: Plant species that were absent in undisturbed portions of the original vegetation of a specific range site and will invade or increase following disturbance or continued heavy grazing (SRM 1999).

Invasive plants: Plants that are not part of (if exotic), or are a minor component of (if native), the original plant community or communities that have the potential to become a dominant or co-dominant species on the site if their future establishment and growth is not actively controlled by management interventions. Species that become dominant for only one to several years (e.g. short-term response to drought or wildfire) are not invasive plants.

Inventory (rangeland inventory): (1) The systematic acquisition and analysis of resource information needed for planning and management of rangeland; (2) the information acquired through rangeland inventory. (SRM 1999).

Life form: Characteristic form or appearance of a species at maturity (e.g., tree, shrub, herb) (SRM 1999).

Litter: The uppermost layer of organic debris on the soil surface, essentially the freshly fallen or slightly decomposed vegetal material (SRM 1999). In this document, it includes persistent and non-persistent organic matter that is in contact with the soil surface.

Microsite: A spatial unit that contains only a few biological individuals that has a distinct climate or soil from the surrounding units (e.g., the spaces between plants relative to the spaces under plants).

Monitoring: The orderly collection, analysis, and interpretation of resource data to evaluate progress toward meeting management objectives. The process must be conducted over time in order to determine whether or not management objectives are being met (SRM 1999).

Native invasive: A native plant that has migrated to a site where it was not a part of the original plant community, or a native plant that because of management or other changes is now increasing beyond its original composition on the site.

Natural disturbance regime: The frequency and intensity of events that occur because of climate or animals (e.g., flood, fire, frost heave, drought, animal burrowing, or defoliation) that alter the structure of ecological systems or the processes that maintain ecological systems.

Nitrogen fixation (fixers): The biological reduction of molecular nitrogen to chemical forms that can be used by organisms in the synthesis of organic molecules.

Normal variability or normal range of variability: The deviation of characteristics of biotic communities and their environment that can be expected given natural variability in climate and disturbance regimes.

Noxious weed: Any plant designated by a Federal, State, or county government to be injurious to public health, agriculture, recreation, wildlife, or any public or private property (Sheley et al. 1999).

Nutrient cycle: The cycle of nutrients, such as nitrogen and phosphorus, through the physical and biotic components of the environment; one of the ecological processes.

Organic matter: Living plant tissue and decomposed or partially decomposed material from living organisms.

Oxidation: The loss of one or more electrons by an ion or molecule (SSSA 1997). Oxidation is a chemical process of decomposition whereby nutrients are released into the atmosphere instead of into the soil. Oxidation commonly increases as aridity increases.

Pedestal (erosional): Plants or rocks that appear elevated as a result of soil loss by wind or water erosion (does not include plant or rock elevation as a result of non-erosional processes such as frost heaving).

Perennial plant: A plant that has a life span of three or more years (USDA 1997).

Physical crust: Thin surface layers induced by impact of raindrops on bare soil causing the soil surface to seal and absorb less water.

Plant decadence: In a plant community, decadence refers to an overabundance of dead or dying plants relative to what is expected for a site given the natural range of variability in disease, climate, and management influences.

Plant mortality: The death of a plant, or in a plant community, the death of a number of plants in the community.

Potential natural community (PNC): The biotic community that would become established on an ecological site if all successional sequences were completed without interferences by man under the present environmental conditions. Natural disturbances are inherent in its development. The PNC may include acclimatized or naturalized nonnative species (USDA 1997).

Potential natural vegetation: A historical term originally defined by A.W. Kuchler as the stable vegetation community which could occupy a site under current climatic conditions without further influence by people. Often used interchangeably with "potential natural community" (SRM 1999).

Preponderance of evidence: The rating of an attribute of rangeland health by observing where the distribution of indicators is in respect to the five categories used to rate each indicator associated with that attribute.

Qualitative data: Observational data derived from visual observations and recorded descriptively but not measured (e.g., descriptive or non-numerical data).

Qualitative rangeland health assessment: The determination of the functional status of attributes through non-numerical observations of indicators. Qualitative assessments have an element of subjectivity.

Quantitative data: Data derived from measurements, such as counts, dimensions, weights, etc., and recorded numerically; may include ratios or other values. Qualitative numerical estimates, such as ocular cover and production estimates, are often referred to as "semi-quantitative."

Quantitative rangeland health assessment: The determination of the functional status of an attribute(s) through measurement of vegetation, soil, or landscape characteristics that are indicators or can be used to derive indicators. Quantitative assessments have a known level of precision and accuracy, and require a quantitative reference.

Range condition: The present status of vegetation of a range site in relation to the climax (natural potential) plant community for that site. It is an expression of the relative degree to which the kinds, proportions, and amounts of plants in a plant community resemble that of the climax plant community for the site (SRM 1999).

Rangeland: Land on which the indigenous vegetation (climax or natural potential) is predominantly grasses, grass-like plants, forbs, or shrubs and is managed as a natural ecosystem. If plants are introduced, they are managed similarly. Rangelands include natural grasslands, savannas, shrublands, many deserts, tundra, alpine communities, marshes, and wet meadows (SRM 1999). The authors of this document also include oak and pinyon-juniper woodlands in this definition.

Rangeland health: The degree to which the integrity of the soil, vegetation, water, and air, as well as the ecological processes of the rangeland ecosystem, are balanced and sustained. Integrity is defined as maintenance of the structure and functional attributes characteristic of a locale, including normal variability (SRM 1999).

Recruitment: The successful entry of new individuals into the breeding population.

Reference state: The reference state is the state where the functional capacities represented by soil/site stability, hydrologic function, and biotic integrity are performing at an optimum level under the natural disturbance regime. This state usually includes, but is not limited to, what is often referred to as the potential natural plant community (PNC). See definition of "State" in Concepts section and Figure 2.

Relative dominance (composition): The percent of cover or production represented by a species or lifeform expressed relative to the total cover or production. It can also be based on biomass.

Relict (area): A remnant or fragment of the climax plant community that remains from a former period when it was more widely distributed. *Synonym:* pristine (SRM 1999).

Resilience: The capacity of ecological processes to recover following a disturbance. Resilience can be defined in terms of the rate of recovery, the extent of recovery during a particular period of time, or both.

Resistance: The capacity of ecological processes to continue to function without change following a disturbance.

Rhizomatous plant: A plant that develops clonal shoots by producing rhizomes. Rhizomes are horizontal underground stems that usually produce roots and shoots from nodes (SRM 1999).

Rill: A small, intermittent water course with steep sides, usually only several centimeters deep (SSSA 1997). Rills generally are linear erosion features.

Runoff: The portion of precipitation or irrigation on an area which does not infiltrate, but instead is discharged by the area (SSSA 1997).

Saltation: A particular type of momentum-dependent transport involving the rolling, bouncing, or jumping action of soil particles 0.1 to 0.5 mm in diameter by wind, usually at a height of <15 cm above the soil surface, for relatively short distances; the rolling, bouncing or jumping action of mineral grains, gravel, stones, or soil aggregates affected by the energy of following water; the bouncing or jumping movement of material downslope in response to gravity (SSSA 1997).

Shrub: A plant that has persistent, woody stems and a relatively low growth habit, and that generally produces several basal shoots instead of a single bole. It differs from a tree by its low stature (generally less than 5 meters, or 16 feet) and non-arborescent form (SRM 1999).

Similarity index (rangeland): The present state of vegetation and soil protection on an ecological site in relation to the historic climax plant community. *Synonym:* range condition. (SRM 1999).

Soil aggregates: A group of primary soil particles that cohere to each other more strongly than to other surrounding particles (SSSA 1997).

Soil association: A kind of map unit used in soil surveys comprised of delineations, each of which shows the size, shape, and location of a landscape unit composed of two or more kinds of component soils or component soils and miscellaneous areas, plus allowable inclusions in either case. The individual bodies of component soils and miscellaneous areas are large enough to be delineated at the scale of 1:24,000. Several bodies of each kind of component soil or miscellaneous area are apt to occur in each delineation, and they occur in a fairly repetitive and describable pattern (SSSA 1997).

Soil classification: The systematic arrangement of soil units into groups or categories on the basis of their characteristics. Broad groupings are made on the basis of general characteristics and subdivisions on the basis of more detailed differences in specific properties (SSSA 1997).

Soil complex: A kind of map unit used in soil surveys comprised of delineations, each of which shows the size, shape, and location of a landscape unit composed of two or more kinds of component soils or component soils and a miscellaneous area, plus allowable inclusions in either case. The individual bodies of component soils and miscellaneous areas are too small to be delineated at the scale of 1:24,000. Several to numerous bodies of each kind of component soil or miscellaneous area are apt to occur in each delineation (SSSA 1997).

Soil inclusions: One or more polypedons or parts of polypedons within a delineation of a map unit, not identified by the map unit name (i.e., is not one of the named component soils or named miscellaneous area components). Such soils or areas are either too small to be delineated separately without creating excessive map or legend detail, occur too erratically to be considered a component, or are not identified by practical mapping methods (SSSA 1997).

Soil/site stability: The capacity of a site to limit redistribution and loss of soil resources (including nutrients and organic matter) by wind and water (one of the three attributes of rangeland health).

Soil structure: The combination or arrangement of primary soil particles into secondary units or peds. The secondary units are characterized on the basis of size, shape, and grade (degree of distinctiveness) (SSSA 1997).

Soil survey: The systematic examination, description, classification, and mapping of soils in an area. Soil surveys are classified according to the kind and intensity of field examination (SSSA 1997).

Soil texture: The relative proportions of the various soil separates (sand, silt, and clay) in a soil (SSSA 1997).

Species composition: The proportions of various plant species in relation to the total on a given area. It may be expressed in terms of cover, density, weight, etc. (SRM 1999).

Standing dead vegetation: The total amount of dead plant material, in aboveground parts, per unit of space, at a given time. (USDA 1997). This component includes all standing dead vegetation produced in the previous (not the current) growing season that is not detached from the plant and is still standing.

State: A state is comprised of an integrated soil and vegetation unit having one or more biological communities that occur on a particular ecological site and that are functionally similar with respect to the three attributes (soil/site stability, hydrologic function, and biotic integrity) under natural disturbance regimes. See Concepts section.

Structure (soils): The combination or arrangement of primary soil particles into secondary units or peds. The secondary units are characterized on the basis of size, shape, and grade (degree of distinctiveness) (SSSA 1997).

Structure (vegetation): The height and area occupied by different plants or life forms in a community.

Subdominant (subordinate) species: Daubenmire (1968) defines subordinate species as "those species, which if removed singly, would not occasion much rearrangement with their ecosystem." For the purposes of this document, *Interpreting Indicators of Rangeland Health*, subdominant plants are those within a community with less size-per-unit area as measured by biomass, production, or cover.

Succulent: Generally a type of cactus.

Terracette: "Benches" of soil deposition behind obstacles caused by water erosion.

Threshold: A transition boundary that an ecosystem crosses resulting in a new stable state that is not easily reversed without significant inputs of resources.

Tiller: A plant shoot that arises from the root or base of a plant.

Transition: A shift between two states. Transitions are not reversible by simply altering the intensity or direction of factors that produced the change. Instead, they require new inputs such as revegetation or shrub removal. Practices, such as these, that accelerate succession (USDA 1997) are often expensive to apply.

Tree: A woody, usually single-stemmed, perennial plant that has a definite crown shape and reaches a mature height of at least 4 meters. The distinction between woody plants, known as trees, and those called shrubs is gradual. Some plants, such as oaks (*Quercus* spp.), may grow as either trees or shrubs (SRM 1999).

Trend: The direction of change in ecological status or resource value rating observed over time (SRM 1999).

Unhealthy rangelands: Rangelands on which degradation has resulted in the loss of ecological processes that function properly, and the capacity to provide values and commodities to a degree that external inputs are required to restore the health of the land (NRC 1994).

Vascular plants: Higher plants with vessels that conduct sap throughout the plant.

Vesicular crust: A type of physical crust that contains numerous small air pockets or spaces similar to a sponge causing a reduction in infiltration.

Viable seed: Wildland plant seed that is capable of germination given appropriate environmental conditions.

Warm season plant: A plant which makes most or all its growth during the spring, summer, and fall, and is usually dormant in winter; a plant that exhibits the C-4 photosynthetic pathway (SRM 1999).

Water cycle: The capture, storage, and redistribution of precipitation. *Synonym:* hydrologic cycle.

Weather: The current state of the atmosphere with regard to wind, temperature, cloudiness, moisture, pressure, etc.

Well-managed rangelands: Rangelands that have properly functioning ecological processes, biotic integrity, and soil stability associated with human uses of the land.

Wind-scoured area: Areas, generally in interspaces, where the finer soil particles have blown away sometimes leaving residual gravel, rock, or exposed roots on the soil surface.

Appendix 1

Evaluation Sheet

Evaluation Sheet (Front)

Aerial Photo:_____

Management Unit:_____ State:_____ Office:_____ Range/Ecol. Site Code:_____
          (Allotment or pasture)

Ecological Site Name:_____ Soil Map Unit/Component Name:_____

Observers:_____ Date:_____

Location (description):_____

T. ____ R. _____   or _____N. Lat.   Or   UTM E_____m   Position by GPS? Y / N
                                                                      UTM Zone___, Datum___

Sec. _____, _____   _____W. Long.   N_____m   Photos taken? Y / N

Size of evaluation area:_____

Composition (Indicators 10 and 12) based on:__Annual Production, __Cover Produced During Current Year or __Biomass

---

Soil/site verification:

Range/Ecol. Site Descr., Soil Surv., and/or Ecol. Ref. Area:	Evaluation Area:
Surface texture _____	Surface texture _____
Depth: very shallow __, shallow __, moderate __, deep __	Depth: very shallow __, shallow __, moderate __, deep __
Type and depth of diagnostic horizons:	Type and depth of diagnostic horizons:

1. _____	3. _____	1. _____	3. _____
2. _____	4. _____	2. _____	4. _____

Surf. Efferv.: none __, v. slight __, slight __, strong __, violent __   Surf. Efferv.: none __, v. slight __, slight __, strong __, violent __

Parent material _____ Slope _____% Elevation _____ft.   Topographic position _____ Aspect _____

Average annual precipitation _____inches   Seasonal distribution _____

Recent weather (last 2 years) (1) drought _____, (2) normal _____, or (3) wet _____.

Wildlife use, livestock use (intensity and season of allotted use), and recent disturbances:
_____
_____
_____
_____

Off-site influences on evaluation area:
_____
_____
_____
_____

Criteria used to select this particular evaluation area as REPRESENTATIVE (specific info. and factors considered; degree of "representativeness")
_____
_____
_____
_____

Other remarks (continue on back if necessary)
_____
_____
_____
_____

Reference: (1) Reference Sheet:_____; Author:_____; Creation Date:_____
or (2) Other (e.g., name and date of ecological site description; locations of ecological reference area(s))_____

Departure from Expected	Code	Instructions for Evaluation Sheet, Page 2
None to Slight	N-S	(1) Assign 17 indicator ratings. If indicator not present, rate None to Slight.
Slight to Moderate	S-M	(2) In the three grids below, write the indicator number in the appropriate column for each indicator that is applicable to the attribute.
Moderate	M	(3) Assign overall rating for each attribute based on preponderance of evidence.
Moderate to Extreme	M-E	(4) Justify each attribute rating in writing.
Extreme to Total	E-T	

Indicator	Rating	Comments
1. Rills	S H	
2. Water-flow Patterns	S H	
3. Pedestals and/or terracettes	S H	
4. Bare ground _____%	S H	
5. Gullies	S H	
6. Wind-scoured, blowouts, and/or deposition areas	S	
7. Litter movement	S	
8. Soil surface resistance to erosion	S H B	
9. Soil surface loss or degradation	S H B	
10. Plant community composition and distribution relative to infiltration	H	
11. Compaction layer	S H B	
12. Functional/structional groups	B	
13. Plant mortality/decadence	B	
14. Litter amount	H B	
15. Annual production	B	
16. Invasive plants	B	
17. Reproductive capability of perennial plants	B	

Attribute Rating Justification
Soil & Site Stability:

E-T	M-E	M	S-M	N-S

S (10 indicators):
Soil & Site Stability
Rating: _____

Attribute Rating Justification
Hydrologic Function:

E-T	M-E	M	S-M	N-S

H (10 indicators):
Hydrologic Function
Rating: _____

Attribute Rating Justification
Biotic Integrity:

E-T	M-E	M	S-M	N-S

B (9 indicators):
Biotic Integrity
Rating: _____

Evaluation Sheet (Example) (Front)

Aerial Photo: _____

Management Unit: <u>Allotment I, pasture I</u> State: <u>NM</u>   Office: <u>Las Cruces</u>   Range/Ecol. Site Code: <u>042XB999NM</u>
(Allotment or pasture)

Ecological Site Name: <u>Limy</u>   Soil Map Unit/Component Name: <u>Nickel gravelly fine sandy loam</u>

Observers: <u>Joe Smith, Jose Garcia, and Thaddeus Jones</u>   Date: <u>June 10, 2002</u>

Location (description): <u>Limy site two miles north of windmill in S.E. pasture</u>

T. <u>11 S</u> R. <u>23 W</u>   or _____ N. Lat.   Or   UTM E _____ m   Position by GPS? Y / N No
                                                                                                                        UTM Zone____, Datum____

Sec. <u>12</u>, <u>NE 1/4</u>   _____ W. Long.   N _____ m   Photos taken? Y / N Yes

Size of evaluation area: <u>Evaluation area is approximately 3 ac. and represents entire ecological site in this pasture</u>

Composition (Indicators 10 and 12) based on: __Annual Production, _X_ Cover Produced During Current Year or __Biomass

Soil/site verification:

Range/Ecol. Site Descr., Soil Surv., and/or Ecol. Ref. Area:	Evaluation Area:
Surface texture <u>grfsl, grlfs, gl</u>	Surface texture <u>gfsl</u>
Depth: very shallow __, shallow __, moderate __, deep _X_	Depth: very shallow __, shallow __, moderate __, deep _X_

Type and depth of diagnostic horizons:
1. <u>Calcic horizon w/in 20"</u>   3. _____
2. _____   4. _____

Type and depth of diagnostic horizons:
1. <u>Calcic horizon at 15"</u>   3. _____
2. _____   4. _____

Surf. Efferv.: none __, v. slight __, slight __, strong _X_, violent __

Surf. Efferv.: none __, v. slight __, slight __, strong _X_, violent __

Parent material <u>Alluvium</u> Slope <u>0-5</u> % Elevation <u>4100</u> ft.   Topographic position <u>toeslope</u>   Aspect <u>south</u>

Average annual precipitation <u>8-12</u> inches   Seasonal distribution <u>Summer thunderstorms dominate</u>

Recent weather (last 2 years) (1) drought _____, (2) normal _X_, or (3) wet _____.

Wildlife use, livestock use (intensity and season of allotted use), and recent disturbances:
<u>Wildlife use is dominated by pronghorn antelope in the winter. Livestock use was extremely heavy yearlong during 1900-1930. Last 50 years, livestock use has been cow/calf moderate yearlong use.</u>
_____
_____

Off-site influences on evaluation area:
<u>None</u>
_____
_____
_____

Criteria used to select this particular evaluation area as REPRESENTATIVE (specific info. and factors considered; degree of "representativeness")
<u>Area is located near a pasture key area. It is located in the center of the ecological site and represents the typical amount of livestock, wildlife and recreational uses on this area. This ecological site dominates this pasture. The area is 3/4 of a mile from the closest water source.</u>
_____
_____

Other remarks (continue on back if necessary)
_____
_____
_____
_____

Reference: (1) Reference Sheet: <u>Limy SD—428</u>   ; Author: <u>J. Christensen</u>   ; Creation Date: <u>03/23/2002</u>
or (2) Other (e.g., name and date of ecological site description; locations of ecological reference area(s)) <u>Limy Ecological Site</u>
<u>042XB999NM, June 2001</u>

Interpreting Indicators of Rangeland Health — Technical Reference 1734-6, Version 4

Departure from Expected	Code	Instructions for Evaluation Sheet, Page 2
None to Slight	N-S	(1) Assign 17 indicator ratings. If indicator not present, rate None to Slight.
Slight to Moderate	S-M	(2) In the three grids below, write the indicator number in the appropriate column for
Moderate	M	each indicator that is applicable to the attribute.
Moderate to Extreme	M-E	(3) Assign overall rating for each attribute based on preponderance of evidence.
Extreme to Total	E-T	(4) Justify each attribute rating in writing.

Indicator	Rating	Comments
1. Rills	S H / M	Active rill formation evident at infrequent intervals
2. Water-flow Patterns	S H / M-E	Flow patterns show cutting and deposition and some connectivity
3. Pedestals and/or terracettes	S H / S-M	Pedestalling in flow patterns only not common
4. Bare ground __48__ %	S H / M	Bare ground rarely connected
5. Gullies	S H / N-S	
6. Wind-scoured, blowouts, and/or deposition areas	S / N S	
7. Litter movement	S / M	Small litter shows sign of moderate movement, larger litter - slight movement
8. Soil surface resistance to erosion	S H B / M-E	Stability values average from 3-4 on surfaces under vegetation canopy and 1-2 in interspaces
9. Soil surface loss or degradation	S H B / M	Severe past erosion has left much of the site without much surface horizon
10. Plant community composition and distribution relative to infiltration	H / M-E	Change from grass dominated to shrub dominated has decreased infiltration and bare ground has increased run-off
11. Compaction layer	S H B / N-S	
12. Functional/structural groups	B / M	Subdominate group basically gone (warm season stoloniferous grass) and Subdominate group (warm season narrow leaf bunchgrass) and Minor group (Evergreen subshrub) have
13. Plant mortality/decadence	B / S M	
14. Litter amount	H B / M-E	Very little litter is on the site for the time of year and rainfall for the year
15. Annual production	B / S M	Production is about 70% of expected
16. Invasive plants	B / N S	
17. Reproductive capability of perennial plants	B / S M	Plants show some signs of stress that will reduce seed production and stolon production this year

Attribute Rating Justification
Soil & Site Stability:

	9			
	7		11	
8	4		6	
2	1	3	5	
E-T	**M-E**	**M**	**S-M**	**N-S**

Although there is some active erosion in flow patterns, most is old and healing. Lots of water leaving the site, but not much erosion. All erosion occuring as concentrated flow.

S (10 indicators): ____
Soil & Site Stability
Rating: __M__

Attribute Rating Justification
Hydrologic Function:

14				
10	9			
8	4		11	
2	1	3	5	
E-T	**M-E**	**M**	**S-M**	**N-S**

Lots of water leaving the site. Runoff is increasing and all litter is being washed away.

H (10 indicators): ____
Hydrologic Function
Rating: __M-E__

Attribute Rating Justification
Biotic Integrity:

		17		
14	12	15	16	
8	9	13	11	
E-T	**M-E**	**M**	**S-M**	**N-S**

Shift in functional structural groups is significant, justifying moderate rating.

B (9 indicators): ____
Biotic Integrity
Rating: __M__

Appendix 2

Reference Sheet

Reference Sheet

Author(s)/participant(s): _____

Contact for lead author: _____

Date: _____ **MLRA:** _____ **Sub-MLRA:** _____ **Ecological Site:** _____ This *must* be verified based on soils and climate (see Ecological Site Description). Current plant community *cannot* be used to identify the ecological site.

Composition (Indicators 10 and 12) based on: __Annual Production, __Foliar Cover, __Biomass

Indicators. For each indicator, describe the potential for the site. Where possible, (1) use numbers, (2) include expected range of values for above- and below-average years and natural disturbance regimes for **each** community within the reference state, when appropriate and (3) cite data. Continue descriptions on separate sheet.

1. Number and extent of rills:

2. Presence of water flow patterns:

3. Number and height of erosional pedestals or terracettes:

4. Bare ground from Ecological Site Description or other studies (rock, litter, lichen, moss, plant canopy are **not** bare ground):

5. Number of gullies and erosion associated with gullies:

6. Extent of wind scoured, blowouts and/or depositional areas:

7. Amount of litter movement (describe size and distance expected to travel):

8. Soil surface (top few mm) resistance to erosion (stability values are averages — most sites will show a range of values):

9. Soil surface structure and SOM content (include type of structure and A-horizon color and thickness):

10. Effect of plant community composition (relative proportion of different functional groups) and spatial distribution on infiltration and runoff:

11. Presence and thickness of compaction layer (usually none; describe soil profile features which may be mistaken for compaction on this site):

12. Functional/Structural Groups (list in order of descending dominance by above-ground production or live foliar cover (specify) using symbols: >>, >, = to indicate much greater than, greater than, and equal to; place dominants, subdominants and "others" on separate lines):
    Dominants:
    Sub-dominants:
    Other:

13. Amount of plant mortality and decadence (include which functional groups are expected to show mortality or decadence):

14. Average percent litter cover (_____%) and depth (_____ inches).

15. Expected annual production (this is TOTAL above-ground production, not just forage production):
    _____ - _____ lbs./acre or kg/ha (choose one)

16. Potential invasive (including noxious) species (native and non-native). List species which BOTH characterize degraded states and have the potential to become a dominant or co-dominant species on the ecological site if their future establishment and growth is not actively controlled by management interventions. Species that become dominant for only one to several years (e.g., short-term response to drought or wildfire) are not invasive plants. Note that unlike other indicators, we are describing what is NOT expected in the reference state for the ecological site.:

17. Perennial plant reproductive capability:

Reference Sheet (Basic Example*)

Author(s)/participant(s): J. Christensen, B. Call, B. Bestelmeyer, R. Placker, D. Trujillo, L. Hauser, D. Coalson, P. Smith, & J. Herrick

Contact for lead author: jchristensen@web.com/334-556-7890

Date: 03/23/2002 **MLRA:** 42 **Sub-MLRA:** _____ **Ecological Site:** Limy _____ This *must* be verified based on soils and climate (see Ecological Site Description). Current plant community *cannot* be used to identify the ecological site.

Composition (Indicators 10 and 12) based on: _X_ Annual Production, __Foliar Cover, __Biomass

Indicators. For each indicator, describe the potential for the site. Where possible, (1) use numbers, (2) include expected range of values for above- and below-average years and natural disturbance regimes for **each** community within the reference state, when appropriate and (3) cite data. Continue descriptions on separate sheet.

1. Number and extent of rills: None

2. Presence of water flow patterns: None, except following extremely high intensity storms, when short (less than 1 m) flow patterns may appear; minimal evidence of past or current soil deposition or erosion.

3. Number and height of erosional pedestals or terracettes: None

4. Bare ground from Ecological Site Description or other studies (rock, litter, lichen, moss, plant canopy are **not** bare ground): 20 – 30 % bare ground; bare patches should be less than 8-10 inch diameter; occasional 12 inch patches associated with shrubs. Larger bare patches also associated with ant mounds and rodent disturbances

5. Number of gullies and erosion associated with gullies: None

6. Extent of wind scoured, blowouts and/or depositional areas: None

7. Amount of litter movement (describe size and distance expected to travel): Minimal and short, associated with water flow patterns following extremely high intensity storms. Litter also may be moved during intense wind storms.

8. Soil surface (top few mm) resistance to erosion (stability values are averages – most sites will show a range of values): Stability class (Herrick et al. 2001) anticipated to be 5-6 at surface and subsurface under vegetation and 4-5 at surface and subsurface in the interspaces. These values need verification at reference sites.

9. Soil surface structure and SOM content (include type and A-horizon color and thickness): 2-4 inch dark brown A horizon with medium granular structure (Otero County Armesa series description refers to platy structure; probably not from a true reference site).

10. Effect of plant community composition (relative proportion of different functional groups) and spatial distribution on infiltration and runoff: High grass canopy and basal cover and small gaps between plants should reduce raindrop impact and slow overland flow, providing increased time for infiltration to occur. High root density of blue grama can limit infiltration. High herbaceous vegetation on this site will result in less rain necessary to sustain this site because more water is retained.

11. Presence and thickness of compaction layer (usually none; describe soil profile features which may be mistaken for compaction on this site): None

12. Functional/Structural Groups (list in order of descending dominance by above-ground production or live cover (specify) using symbols: >>, >, = to indicate much greater than, greater than, and equal to; place dominants, subdominants and "others" on separate lines):
    Dominants: Blue grama > Black grama >
    Sub-dominants: warm season bunchgrasses > Yucca = shrubs >>
    Other: sub-shrubs = succulents; Forbs 0 – 8 % depending on the year.

13. Amount of plant mortality and decadence (include which functional groups are expected to show mortality or decadence): Grasses will nearly always show some mortality and decadence

14. Average percent litter cover (_____%) and depth (_____ inches). 20 – 25 % litter cover and 0.25 inch depth

15. Expected annual production (this is TOTAL above-ground production, not just forage production): _____ - _____ #/acre or kg/ha (choose one) 650 to 1200 pounds/acre based on ecological site description. Could be even higher on particularly good years.

16. Potential invasive (including noxious) species (native and non-native). List species which BOTH characterize degraded states and have the potential to become a dominant or co-dominant species on the ecological site if their future establishment and growth is not actively controlled by management interventions. Species that become dominant for only one to several years (e.g., short-term response to drought or wildfire) are not invasive plants. Note that unlike other indicators, we are describing what is NOT expected in the reference state for the ecological site.: Possibly creosote bush which is an invader on similar ecological sites; snakeweed is cyclical, so not regarded as an invasive plant on this ecological site.

17. Perennial plant reproductive capability: all species should be capable of reproducing

*This example includes he absolute minimum information required. Ideally, Reference Sheets should include at least as much info mation as is included in he "Standard Example" on the next page.

Reference Sheet (Standard Example)

Author(s)/participant(s): <u>Winnemucca Class Participants (May 12-15, 2005)</u>

Contact for lead author: _____ **Reference site used?** <u>Yes</u>

Date: <u>5/11/05</u> **MLRA:** <u>024XY</u> **Ecological Site:** <u>Loamy 8-10" PZ, 024XY005NV.</u> This *must* be verified based on soils and climate (see Ecological Site Description). Current plant community cannot be used to identify the ecological site.

Composition (indicators 10 and 12) based on: <u>X</u> Annual Production, __Foliar Cover, __Biomass

Indicators. For each indicator, describe the potential for the site. Where possible, (1) use numbers, (2) include expected range of values for above- and below-average years for **each** community and natural disturbance regimes within the reference state, when appropriate and (3) cite data. Continue descriptions on separate sheet.

1. **Number and extent of rills:** Minimal on slopes less than 10% and increasing slightly as slopes increase up to 50%. Rills spaced 15-50 feet apart when present on slopes of 10-50%. After wildfires, high levels of natural herbivory or extended drought, or combinations of these disturbances, rills may double in numbers on slopes from 10-50% after high intensity summer thunderstorms.

2. **Presence of water flow patterns:** Generally up to 20 feet apart and short (less than 10 feet long) with numerous obstructions that alter the water flow path. On slopes of 10-50%, flow patterns increase in number and length. Flow pattern length and numbers may double after wildfires, high levels of natural herbivory, extended drought, or combinations of these disturbances if high intensity summer thunderstorms occur.

3. **Number and height of erosional pedestals or terracettes:** Plant or rock pedestals and terracettes are almost always in flow patterns. Wind caused pedestals are rare and only would be on the site after wildfires, high levels of natural herbivory, extended drought, or combinations of these disturbances. Pedestals of Sandberg bluegrass on pedestals outside water flow patterns are generally caused by frost heaving, not erosion. Pedestals and terracettes would be particularly apparent on 10-50% slopes, especially immediately after high intensity summer thunderstorms.

4. **Bare ground from Ecological Site Description or other studies (rock, litter, standing dead, lichen, moss, plant canopy are not bare ground):** 10-20% or less bare ground with bare patches less than 10% of the evaluation area occurring as intercanopy patches larger than 2 feet in diameter (intercanopy patches can include areas that are not bare ground). Most large patches can include areas that are not bare ground. Within this range, lower slopes are expected to have less bare ground than steeper slopes. Upper end of precip range (10") will also have less bare ground. Canopy gaps generally less than 12 inches in diameter in the intervals between natural disturbance events. Bare ground would be expected to increase to 80% or more the first year following wildfire but to decrease to prefire levels within 2-5 years depending on climate and other disturbances. Multi-year droughts can also cause bare ground to increase to 30%.

5. **Number of gullies and erosion associated with gullies:** Gullies are rare and would only be present when a high intensity summer thunderstorm occurs after wildfires, with high levels of natural herbivory, extended drought, or combinations of these disturbances.

6. **Extent of wind scoured, blowouts and/or depositional areas:** Wind erosion is minimal. Moderate wind erosion can occur when disturbances such as severe wildfires, high levels of natural herbivory, extended drought, or combinations of these disturbances. After rain events, exposed soil surfaces form a physical crust that tends to reduce wind erosion.

7. **Amount of litter movement (describe size and distance expected to travel):** Litter movement consists primarily of redistribution of fine litter (herbaceous plant material) in flow patterns for distances of 1-3 feet on 2-15% slopes, 4-6 feet on 15-30% slopes, and 7-10 feet on 30-50% slopes. After wildfires, high levels of natural herbivory, extended drought, or combinations of these disturbances, size of litter and distance litter moves can increase with coarse woody litter and fine litter moving up to 10' (2-15% slope); 25' (15-30% slope); 100' (30-50% slope).

8. **Soil surface (top few mm) resistance to erosion (stability values are averages – most sites will show a range of values):** Values of 4.5-5.5 under canopies and in intercanopy spaces.

9. **Soil surface structure and SOM content (include type and strength of structure, and A-horizon color and thickness):** Surface layer is light brown and 6-7 inches thick with moderate granular structure. Loss of several millimeters of soil may occur immediately after a high intensity wildfire, high levels of natural herbivory, extended drought, or combinations of these disturbances.

10. **Effect of plant community composition (relative proportion of different functional groups) and spatial distribution on infiltration and runoff:** Perennial plants and especially sagebrush capture snow, increasing soil water availability in the spring. High bunchgrass density increases infiltration by improving soil structure and slowing runoff. Loss of sagebrush after a high intensity wildfire reduces snow accumulation in the winter, reducing the depth of soil water recharge negatively affecting growth and production of deep rooted forbs and perennial grasses. This reduced soil water recharge is part of the site dynamics if exotics or other management actions don't delay the succession back to a sagebrush-grass plant community.

11. **Presence and thickness of compaction layer (usually none; describe soil profile features which may be mistaken for compaction on this site):** Compaction layers should not be present. There are soil profile features in the top 8 inches of the soil profile that would be mistaken for a management induced soil compaction layer. Silica accumulations can cause denser horizons; however these horizons can be distinguished from compaction by their brittleness and "shiny" material in the horizon. These silica accumulations will increase the hardness of the soil, but compaction can still occur and be detected as degradation of soil structure and loss of macropores.

12. **Functional/Structural Groups (list in order of descending dominance by above-ground weight using symbols: >>, >, = to indicate much greater than, greater than, and equal to) with dominants and sub-dominants and "others" on separate lines:**
    Dominant: mid+tall grasses > non-sprouting shrubs (except following fire, when non-resprouting shrubs become rare on the site)
    Sub-dominant: shortgrasses > sprouting shrubs
    Other: annual forbs, perennial forbs
    Biological crust will be present with lichen + moss cover of 10–15%
    After wildfires the functional/structural dominance changes to the herbaceous components with a slow 10-20 year recovery of the non resprouting shrubs (e.g., big sagebrush). Resprouting shrubs tend to increase until the sagebrush reestablishment and increase reduces the resprouting component. High levels of natural herbivory, extended drought, or combinations of these factors can increase shrub functional/structural groups at the expense of the herbaceous groups and biological crust.

13. **Amount of plant mortality and decadence (include which functional groups are expected to show mortality or decadence):** Most of the perennial plants in this community are long lived, especially the perennial forbs and shrubs. After moderate to high intensity wildfires, all of the non-resprouting shrubs would die as would a small percentage of the herbaceous understory species. Extended droughts would tend to cause relatively high mortality in short lived species such as bottlebrush squirreltail and Sandberg bluegrass. Shrub mortality would be limited to severe, multiple year droughts. Combinations of wildfires and extended droughts would cause even more mortality for several years following the fire than either disturbance functioning by itself. Up to 20% dead branches on sagebrush following drought alone.

14. **Average percent litter cover (20%) and depth (1/4" inches)** After wildfires, high levels of natural herbivory, extended drought, or combinations of these disturbances, litter cover and depth decreases to none immediately after the disturbance (e.g., fire) and dependent on climate and plant production increases to post-disturbance levels in one to five growing seasons.

15. **Expected annual production (this is TOTAL above-ground production, not just forage production):** 400 lbs/ac in low precip years, 600 lbs/ac in average precip years and 800 lbs/ac in above average precip years #/acre. After wildfires, high levels of natural herbivory, extended drought, or combinations of these disturbances, can cause production to be significantly reduced (100-200 lbs per ac. the first growing season following a wildfire) and recover slowly under below average precipitation regimes.

16. **Potential invasive (including noxious) species (native and non-native). List species which BOTH characterize degraded states and have the potential to become a dominant or co-dominant species on the ecological site if their future establishment and growth is not actively controlled by management interventions. Species that become dominant for only one to several years (e.g., short-term response to drought or wildfire) are not invasive plants. Note that unlike other indicators, we are describing what is NOT expected in the reference state for the ecological site.:** Cheatgrass is the greatest threat to dominate this site after disturbance (primarily wildfires but disturbances also include high levels of natural herbivory and/or extended drought). Exotic mustards and Russian thistle may dominate soon after disturbance but are eventually replaced as dominants by cheatgrass. Hoary cress, Russian knapweed, bur buttercup and tall whitetop may meet the definition of an invasive species for this site in the future, but do not currently meet the criteria of being a threat to dominate the site after the disturbance.

17. **Perennial plant reproductive capability:** Only limitations to reproductive capability are weather-related and natural disease or herbivory that reduces reproductive capability.

Appendix 3

Functional/Structural Groups Sheet

Functional/Structural Groups Sheet

State _____ Office _____ Ecological Site _____ Site ID _____

Observers _____ Date _____

Functional/Structural Groups			Species List for Functional/Structural Groups
Name	Potential[1]	Actual[2]	Plant Names
Noxious Weeds			
Invasive Plants			
Biological Crust[3]			

Indicate whether each "structural/functional group" is a Dominant (D) (roughly 40-100 % composition), **a Sub-dominant (S)** (roughly 10-40% composition) **a Minor Component (M)** (roughly 2-10% composition), or **a Trace Component (T)** (<2% composition) based on weight or cover composition in the area of interest (e.g., "Actual[2]" column) relative to the "Potential[1]" column derived from information found in the ecological site/description and/or at the ecological reference area.

Biological Crust[3] dominance is evaluated solely on cover, not composition by weight.

78

Interpreting Indicators of Rangeland Health — Technical Reference 1734-6, Version 4

Functional/Structural Groups Sheet (Example)

State NM   **Office** Las Cruces   **Ecological Site** Limy   **Site ID** 042XB999NM

Observers Smith, Garcia and Jones   **Date** 6/10/2002

Functional/Structural Groups			Species List for Functional/Structural Groups
Name	Potential[1]	Actual[2]	Plant Names
Warm season bunchgrasses	D	S	blue grama, plains bristlegrass, cane bluestem
Warm season stoloniferous grasses	S	T	black grama
Warm season narrow leaf bunchgrasses	S	D	dropseeds spp, threeawn spp.
Yucca	M	M	yucca spp.
Evergreen sub-shrub	M	D	broom snakeweed
Perennial taprooted forbs	M	M	globemallow, desert marigold, croton
Annual forbs	T	T	buckwheat, lambsquarter
Annual grasses	T	T	fluff grass, sixweeks grama
Noxious Weeds			
Invasive Plants			
Biological Crust[3] T T			

Indicate whether each "structural/functional group" is a Dominant (D) (roughly 40-100 % composition), **a Sub-dominant (S)** (roughly 10-40% composition) **a Minor Component (M)** (roughly 2-5% composition), or **a Trace Component (T)** (<2% composition) based on weight or cover composition in the area of interest (e.g., "Actual[2]" column) relative to the "Potential[1]" column derived from information found in the ecological site/description and/or at the ecological reference area.

Biological Crust[3] dominance is evaluated solely on cover, not composition by weight.

Appendix 4

Evaluation Matrix

Evaluation Matrix

State _____ Office _____ Ecological Site _____ Site ID _____

Authors _____ Revision Date _____

Departure from Reference Sheet

Indicator*	Extreme to Total	Moderate to Extreme	Moderate	Slight to Moderate	None to Slight
1. Rills _____	_____	_____	_____	_____	Reference Sheet: ____
Generic Descriptor	Rill formation is severe and well defined throughout most of the site.	Rill formation is moderately active and well defined throughout most of the site.	Active rill formation is slight at infrequent intervals; mostly in exposed areas.	No recent formation of rills; old rills have blunted or muted features.	Current or past formation of rills as expected for the site.
2. Water Flow Patterns _____	_____	_____	_____	_____	Reference Sheet: ____
Generic Descriptor	Water flow patterns extensive and numerous; unstable with active erosion; usually connected.	Water flow patterns more numerous and extensive than expected; deposition and cut areas common; occasionally connected.	Number and length of water flow patterns nearly match what is expected for the site; erosion is minor with some instability and deposition.	Number and length of water flow patterns match what is expected for the site; some evidence of minor erosion. Flow patterns are stable and short.	Matches what is expected for the site; minimal evidence of past or current soil deposition or erosion.
3. Pedestals and/or Terracettes _____	_____	_____	_____	_____	Reference Sheet: ____
Generic Descriptor	Abundant active pedestalling and numerous terracettes. Many rocks and plants are pedestaled; exposed plant roots are common.	Moderate active pedestalling; terracettes common. Some rocks and plants are pedestaled with occasional exposed roots.	Slight active pedestalling; most pedestals are in flow paths and interspaces and/or on exposed slopes. Occasional terracettes present.	Active pedestalling or terracette formation is rare; some evidence of past pedestal formation, especially in water flow patterns on exposed slopes.	Current or past evidence of pedestaled plants or rocks as expected for the site. Terracettes absent or uncommon.

* Descriptions for each indicator should be more specific than those listed in the Generic Descriptors, if possible, and refer to the criteria included in the None to Slight description, which is based on the Reference Sheet (Appendix 1).

Indicator*	Extreme to Total	Moderate to Extreme	Moderate	Slight to Moderate	None to Slight
4. Bare Ground ___	_____	_____	_____	_____	Reference Sheet: ___
Generic Descriptor	Much higher than expected for the site. Bare areas are large and generally connected.	Moderate to much higher than expected for the site. Bare areas are large and occasionally connected.	Moderately higher than expected for the site. Bare areas are of moderate size and sporadically connected.	Slightly to moderately higher than expected for the site. Bare areas are small and rarely connected.	Amount and size of bare areas match that expected for the site.
5. Gullies _____	_____	_____	_____	_____	Reference Sheet: ___
Generic Descriptor	Common with indications of active erosion and downcutting; vegetation is infrequent on slopes and/or bed. Nickpoints and headcuts are numerous and active.	Moderate in number to common with indications of active erosion; vegetation is intermittent on slopes and/or bed. Headcuts are active; down-cutting is not apparent.	Moderate in number with indications of active erosion; vegetation is intermittent on slopes and/or bed. Occasional headcuts may be present.	Uncommon, vegetation is stabilizing the bed and slopes; no signs of active headcuts, nickpoints, or bed erosion.	Match what is expected for the site; drainages are represented as natural stable channels; vegetation common and no signs of erosion.
6. Wind Scoured, Blowout, and/or Depositional Areas	_____	_____	_____	_____	Reference Sheet: ___
Generic Descriptor	Extensive.	Common.	Occasionally present.	Infrequent and few.	Match what is expected for the site.

* Descriptions for each indicator should be more specific than those listed in the Generic Descriptors, if possible, and refer to the criteria included in the None to Slight description, which is based on the Reference Sheet (Appendix 1).

Departure from Reference Sheet

Indicator*	Extreme to Total	Moderate to Extreme	Moderate	Slight to Moderate	None to Slight
7. Litter Movement (wind or water) _____					Reference Sheet: _____
Generic Descriptor	Extreme; concentrated around obstructions. Most size classes of litter have been displaced.	Moderate to extreme; loosely concentrated near obstructions. Moderate to small size classes of litter have been displaced.	Moderate movement of smaller size classes in scattered concentrations around obstructions and in depressions.	Slightly to moderately more than expected for the site with only small size classes of litter being displaced.	Matches that expected for the site with a fairly uniform distribution of litter.
8. Soil Surface Resistance to Erosion _____					Reference Sheet: _____
Generic Descriptor	Extremely reduced throughout the site. Biological stabilization agents including organic matter and biological crusts virtually absent.	Significantly reduced in most plant canopy interspaces and moderately reduced beneath plant canopies. Stabilizing agents present only in isolated patches.	Significantly reduced in at least half of the plant canopy interspaces, or moderately reduced throughout the site.	Some reduction in soil surface stability in plant interspaces or slight reduction throughout the site. Stabilizing agents reduced below expected.	Matches that expected for the site. Surface soil is stabilized by organic matter decomposition products and/or a biological crust.
9. Soil Surface Loss or Degradation _____					Reference Sheet: _____
Generic Descriptor	Soil surface horizon absent. Soil structure near surface is similar to, or more degraded, than that in subsurface horizons. No distinguishable difference in subsurface organic matter content.	Soil loss or degradation severe throughout site. Minimal differences in soil organic matter content and structure of surface and subsurface layers.	Moderate soil loss or degradation in plant interspaces with some degradation beneath plant canopies. Soil structure is degraded and soil organic matter content is significantly reduced.	Some soil loss has occurred and/or soil structure shows signs of degradation, especially in plant interspaces.	Soil surface horizon intact. Soil structure and organic matter content match that expected for site.

* Descriptions for each indicator should be more specific than those listed in the Generic Descriptors, if possible, and refer to the criteria included in the None to Slight description, which is based on the Reference Sheet (Appendix 1).

Indicator*	Extreme to Total	Moderate to Extreme	Moderate	Slight to Moderate	None to Slight
10. Plant Community Composition and Distribution Relative to Infiltration and Runoff	_____ _____ _____ _____ _____	_____ _____ _____ _____ _____	_____ _____ _____ _____ _____	_____ _____ _____ _____ _____	Reference Sheet:_____ _____ _____ _____ _____
	_____ _____ _____ _____ _____	_____ _____ _____ _____ _____	_____ _____ _____ _____ _____	_____ _____ _____ _____ _____	_____ _____ _____ _____ _____
Generic Descriptor	Infiltration is severely decreased due to adverse changes in plant community composition and/or distribution. Adverse plant cover changes have occurred.	Infiltration is greatly decreased due to adverse changes in plant community composition and/or distribution. Detrimental plant cover changes have occurred.	Infiltration is moderately reduced due to adverse changes in plant community composition and/or distribution. Plant cover changes negatively affect infiltration.	Infiltration is slightly to moderately affected by minor changes in plant community composition and/or distribution. Plant cover changes have only a minor effect on infiltration.	Infiltration and runoff are not affected by any changes in plant community composition and distribution. Any changes in infiltration and runoff can be attributed to other factors (e.g. compaction).
11. Compaction Layer (below soil surface) _____	_____ _____ _____ _____ _____	_____ _____ _____ _____ _____	_____ _____ _____ _____ _____	_____ _____ _____ _____ _____	Reference Sheet:_____ _____ _____ _____ _____
	_____ _____ _____ _____	_____ _____ _____ _____	_____ _____ _____ _____	_____ _____ _____ _____	_____ _____ _____ _____
Generic Descriptor	Extensive; severely restricts water movement and root penetration.	Widespread; greatly restricts water movement and root penetration.	Moderately widespread, moderately restricts water movement and root penetration.	Rarely present or is thin and weakly restrictive to water movement and root penetration.	Matches that expected for the site; none to minimal, not restrictive to water movement and root penetration.

* Descriptions for each indicator should be more specific than those listed in the Generic Descriptors, if possible, and refer to the criteria included in the None to Slight description, which is based on the Reference Sheet (Appendix 1).

Departure from Reference Sheet

Indicator*	Extreme to Total	Moderate to Extreme	Moderate	Slight to Moderate	None to Slight
12. Functional/ Structural Groups (F/S Groups) See Functional/ Structural Groups Worksheet					Reference Sheet:____
Generic Descriptor	Number of F/S groups greatly reduced **and/or** Relative dominance of F/S groups has been dramatically altered **and/or** Number of species within F/S groups dramatically reduced.	Number of F/S groups reduced **and/or** One dominant group and/or one or more sub-dominate group replaced by F/S groups not expected for the site **and/or** Number of species within F/S groups significantly reduced.	Number of F/S groups moderately reduced **and/or** One or more sub-dominant F/S groups replaced by F/S groups not expected for the site **and/or** Number of species within F/S groups moderately reduced.	Number of F/S groups slightly reduced **and/or** Relative dominance of F/S groups has been modified from that expected for the site **and/or** number of species within F/S slightly reduced.	F/S groups and number of species in each group closely match that expected for the site.
13. Plant Mortality/ Decadence _____					Reference Sheet:____
Generic Descriptor	Dead and/or decadent plants are common.	Dead plants and/or decadent plants are somewhat common.	Some dead and/or decadent plants are present.	Slight plant mortality and/or decadence.	Plant mortality and decadence match that expected for the site.
14. Litter Amount					Reference Sheet:____
Generic Descriptor	Largely absent or dominant relative to site potential and weather.	Greatly reduced or increased relative to site potential and weather.	Moderately more or less relative to site potential and weather.	Slightly more or less relative to site potential and weather.	Amount is what is expected for the site potential and weather.

* Descriptions for each indicator should be more specific than those listed in the Generic Descriptors, if possible, and refer to the criteria included in the None to Slight description, which is based on the Reference Sheet (Appendix 1).

Indicator*	Extreme to Total	Moderate to Extreme	Moderate	Slight to Moderate	None to Slight
15. Annual Production ____	_____	_____	_____	_____	Reference Sheet:____
	_____	_____	_____	_____	_____
	_____	_____	_____	_____	_____
	_____	_____	_____	_____	_____
	_____	_____	_____	_____	_____
Generic Descriptor	Less than 20% of potential production for the site based on recent weather.	20-40% of potential production for the site based on recent weather.	40-60% of potential production for the site based on recent weather.	60-80% of potential production for the site based on recent weather.	Exceeds 80% of potential production for the site based on recent weather.
16. Invasive Plants	_____	_____	_____	_____	Reference Sheet:____
	_____	_____	_____	_____	_____
	_____	_____	_____	_____	_____
	_____	_____	_____	_____	_____
Generic Descriptor	Dominate the site.	Common throughout the site.	Scattered throughout the site.	Present primarily in disturbed areas within the site.	If present, composition of invasive species, matches that expected for the site.
17. Reproductive Capability of Perennial Plants (native or seeded)	_____	_____	_____	_____	Reference Sheet: ____
	_____	_____	_____	_____	_____
	_____	_____	_____	_____	_____
	_____	_____	_____	_____	_____
	_____	_____	_____	_____	_____
	_____	_____	_____	_____	_____
	_____	_____	_____	_____	_____
Generic Descriptor	Capability to produce seed or vegetative tillers is severely reduced relative to recent climatic conditions.	Capability to produce seed or vegetative tillers is greatly reduced relative to recent climatic conditions	Capability to produce seed or vegetative tillers is moderately reduced relative to recent climatic conditions.	Capability to produce seed or vegetative tillers is slightly reduced relative to recent climatic conditions.	Capability to produce seed or vegetative tillers is not reduced relative to recent climatic conditions.

* Descriptions for each indicator should be more specific than those listed in the Generic Descriptors, if possible, and refer to the criteria included in the None to Slight description, which is based on the Reference Sheet (Appendix 1).

Appendix 5
Photographs of the 17 Indicators

1. Rills

1a - Rills are a natural component of this site due to erodible soils.

1b - Short linear rill caused by accelerated water flow.

2. Water Flow Patterns

2a - Extensive water flow pattern in plant interspace indicative of high overland water flow.

2b - Short water flow pattern (white dotted line) in plant interspaces.

3. Pedestals and/or Terracettes

3a - Plant pedestal caused by wind erosion. Note the exposed roots (arrow).

3b - Terracette (arrow) caused by litter obstruction in water flow pattern.

3. Pedestals and/or Terracettes (continued)

3c - Terraces formed by ungulate grazing on hillsides are not evaluated with this indicator. Other indicators that may be applicable in this situation include numbers 4, 8, 9, and 11.

4. Bare Ground

4a - Amount of bare ground is slight relative to site potential and recent weather.

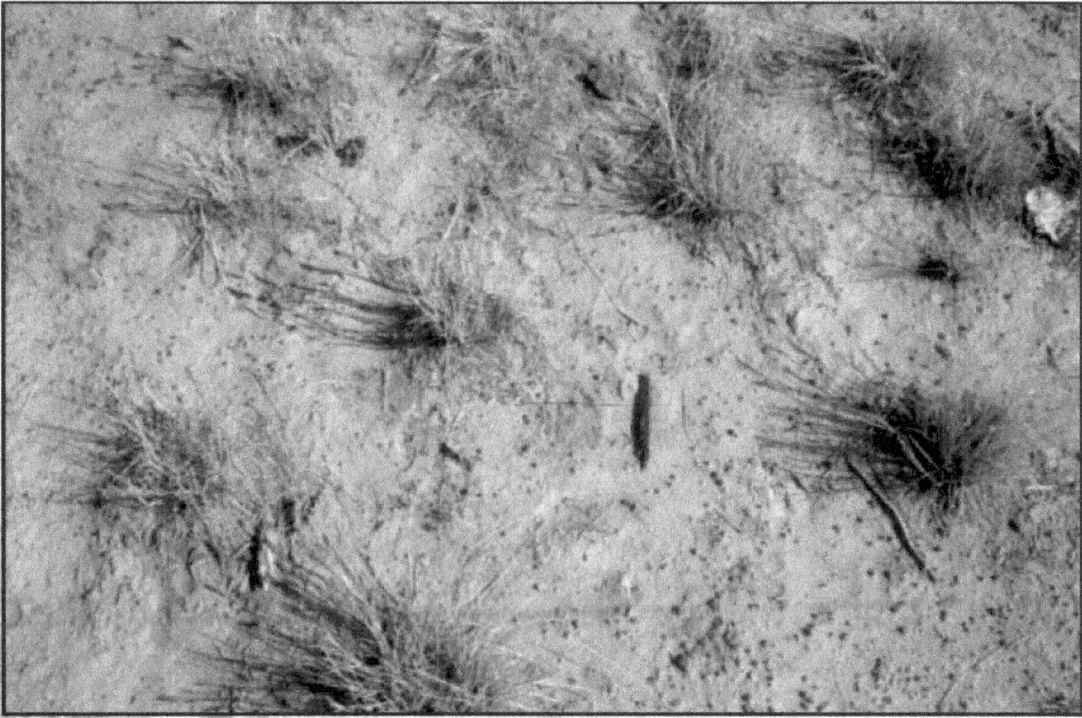

4b - Amount of bare ground is excessive relative to site potential and recent weather.

5. Gullies

5a - Gully that shows signs of active erosion (nickpoints - see arrows) and downcutting.

5b - Relatively stable gully with few signs of active erosion with good vegetation recovery occurring.

6. Wind-Scoured, Blowouts, and/or Deposition Areas

6a - Wind-scoured areas in plant interspaces (star) with soil and litter deposition occurring at plant bases (arrows).

7. Litter Movement

7a - Litter movement and accumulation in a water flow pattern.

7b - Litter redistributed by wind under shrub canopy and around obstructions in the interspaces.

8. Soil Surface Resistance to Erosion

8a - Surface physical crusts in plant interspaces can increase overland flow of water.

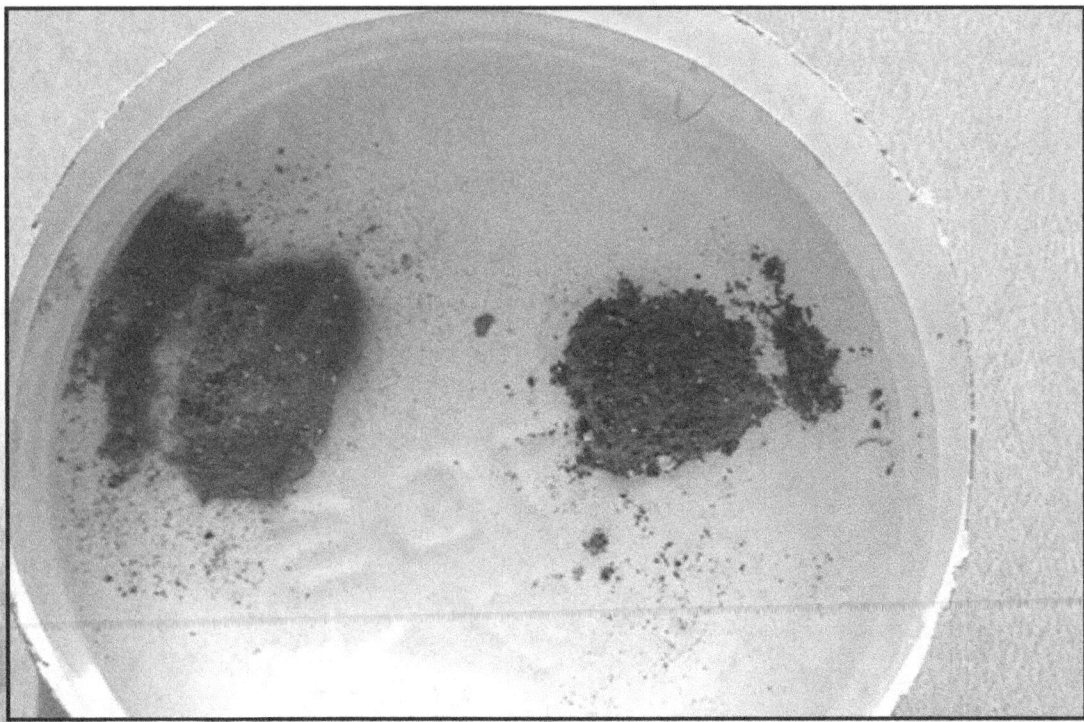

8b - Soil surface fragment on right is resistant to breakdown in water indicating presence of soil-binding organic matter. Soil surface fragment on left is "melting" indicating less organic matter and stability.

9. Soil Surface Loss or Degradation

9a - Evidence of soil surface loss (foreground) is evident when compared to the cover of the plant and biological crust in the background.

10. Plant Community Composition and Distribution Relative to Infiltration and Runoff

10a - Desert grassland site where grasses promote infiltration and minimize runoff.

10b - Degraded desert grassland site where runoff has dramatically increased due to conversion from grass to shrubs.

11. Compaction Layer

11a - An example of a restrictive compaction layer that reduces root penetration and water percolation.

12. Functional/Structural Groups

12a - Nitrogen-fixing forb (*Astragalus* spp.) that is included in a different functional group than non-nitrogen-fixing forbs.

12b - Biological crusts (foreground) are an important functional/structural component in many plant communities.

12. Functional/Structural Groups (continued)

12c - Sagebrush-perennial bunchgrass site near potential. Native annual grasses are a minor component of the vegetation mix.

12d - Perennial bunchgrasses have been replaced with cheatgrass, an exotic annual grass. Accelerated erosion is also evident.

13. Plant Mortality/Decadence

13a - Dead and decadent sagebrush (*Artemisia* spp.) plants.

13b - Decadent shrub with dead branches.

14. Litter Amount

14a - Amount of litter is in balance with site potential and recent weather.

14b - Litter is uncommon compared to what is expected given the site potential and recent weather.

14. Litter Amount (continued)

14c - Amount of litter and standing dead vegetation is well above what is expected due to the presence of an exotic annual grass.

15. Annual Production

15a - Production of current year's aboveground biomass is consistent with site potential and recent weather.

15b - Production of current year's aboveground biomass is well below site potential relative to recent weather.

16. Invasive Plants

16a - Cheatgrass (*Bromus tectorum*) is an exotic invasive annual grass that can dominate the understory in disturbed shrublands.

16b - State-listed noxious weeds, such as this knapweed in Idaho, are another category of invasive plants.

16. Invasive Plants (continued)

16c - Juniper, a native tree, is invasive when it invades rangeland sites where the potential is for shrubs and herbaceous plants.

17. Reproductive Capability of Perennial Plants

17a - Perennial forbs and grasses show good potential for reproduction as evidenced by flowers and seed-stalk production.

17b - Reproduction potential of this shrub is low due to lack of seed production.

Appendix 6

Quantitative Measures for the 17 Indicators

Quantitative Measures for the 17 Indicators

Potential quantitative measurements and indicators that we believe specifically relate to the 17 rangeland health qualitative indicators. For each quantitative indicator, we provide a potential explanation (interpretation) of the relationship between the qualitative and quantitative indicators (from Pyke et al., 2002). Also see table relating quantitative indicators to attributes in the Concepts section. References: 1 - USDA NRCS, 1997, 2 - Elzinga et al., 2001, 3 - Herrick et al., 2002.

Qualitative Indicator	Quantitative Indicator	Measurement (References)	Interpretation
1. Rills	None		
2. Water flow patterns	Percent basal cover	Line-point intercept (2,3)	Basal cover is *negatively* correlated with water flow patterns because plant bases slow water movement.
	Proportion of basal gaps > 25, 50, 100, 200 cm	Basal gap intercept (3)	Basal gaps are *positively* correlated with water flow patterns because water gains energy as it moves unobstructed across larger gaps.
3. Pedestals and/or terracettes	Standard deviation of pin heights	Erosion bridge (microtopography) (3)	Pedestals and terracettes *can be positively* correlated with pin height standard deviation because increased microtopography is *sometimes* due to pedestals and terracettes.
4. Bare ground	Percent bare ground	Line-point intercept (2,3)	Bare ground is *positively* correlated with runoff and erosion.
	Proportion of line in canopy gaps > 25, 50, 100, 200 cm	Canopy gap intercept (3)	The bare ground qualitative indicator is also *positively* correlated with canopy gaps because bare ground in large gaps usually has a larger effect on many functions than bare ground in small gaps.
5. Gullies	Width-to-depth ratio and side slope angle	Channel profiles (3)	Lower width-to-depth ratios and higher side slope angles both reflect more severe or active gully erosion.
	Headcut movement	Headcut location (3)	Higher rates of headcut movement reflect greater gully erosion.
6. Wind-scoured, blowout, and/or depositional areas	None		
7. Litter movement	Proportion of litter cover in interspaces vs. under canopies	Line-point intercept (2,3)	Higher proportions of litter in the interspaces can be *positively* related to litter movement.
	Proportion of basal gaps > 25, 50, 100, 200 cm	Basal gap intercept (3)	Basal gaps can be *positively* related to redistribution or loss of litter.
8. Soil surface resistance to erosion	Average soil surface stability	Soil stability kit (surface)(3)	Surface aggregate stability is *positively* related to soil's resistance to wind and water erosion.
9. Soil surface loss or degradation	Average soil sub-surface stability	Soil stability kit (sub-surface)(3)	Sub-surface soil structure degrades and organic matter declines as surface soil is lost, thus sub-surface aggregate stability is negatively related to soil surface loss or degradation.
10. Plant community composition and distribution relative to infiltration and runoff.	Percent composition	Line-point intercept (2,3) or production (1,2)	Changes in species composition can be related to changes in infiltration. For example, root and shoot morphology of tussock vs. stoloniferous plants.
	Proportion of basal gaps > 25, 50, 100, 200 cm	Basal gap intercept (3)	Changes in basal gaps can be related to changes plant distributions that relate to infiltration and runoff.
11. Compaction layer	Ratio of penetration resistance in the upper 15 cm (6 inches) between the evaluation and reference area	Impact penetrometer (3)	Ratios of penetration resistance or bulk density above 1 can indicate the presence of a compaction layer.
	Ratio of mass-per-volume of soil in the upper 15 cm between the evaluation and reference area	Bulk density	
12. Functional/structural groups	Percent composition by functional or structural group and group richness	Line-point intercept (2,3) Production (1,2)	Composition and richness of functional or structural groups are *positively* related to plant functional or structural groups qualitative indicator
13. Plant mortality/decadence	Proportion of live-to-dead canopy	Line-point intercept (2,3)	The live-to-dead proportion is *positively* related to the plant mortality or decadence qualitative indicator
14. Litter amount	Litter mass	Litter mass	The amount of litter mass and cover per unit area is related to litter amount.
	Litter cover	Line-point intercept (2,3)	
15. Annual production	Total annual production	Production (1,2)	Productions relates directly with the qualitative indicator of annual production
16. Invasive plants	Density of invasive species	Belt transect (1,2,3)	Number of species and their densities or cover will directly relate to the qualitative indicator
	Percent foliar cover of invasive species	Line-point intercept (2,3), Production (1,2), or quadrat cover (1,2)	
17. Reproductive capability of perennial plants	None		

Appendix 7

Soil Stability Kit

Table 1. Soil Stability Evaluation for 1/4"-diameter Air-Dry Samples

ALWAYS Sieve Soils (even if rated ≤ 3) to Verify Class

Stability class	Criteria for assignment to stability class (for Standard Characterization)[e]
1	**50%** of structural integrity lost within **5 seconds** of insertion in water OR too unstable to sample (falls through sieve)*.
2	**50%** of structural integrity lost **5–30 seconds** after insertion.
3	**50%** of structural integrity lost **30–300 seconds** after insertion or <10% of soil remains on sieve after 5 dipping cycles.
4	**10 - 25%** of soil remains on sieve after 5 dipping cycles.
5	**25 - 75%** of soil remains on sieve after 5 dipping cycles.
6	**75 - 100%** of soil remains on sieve after 5 dipping cycles.

* If too unstable to sample, try gently wetting with a mister (perfume bottle available at drug stores), remove sample, and allow to air-dry before testing.

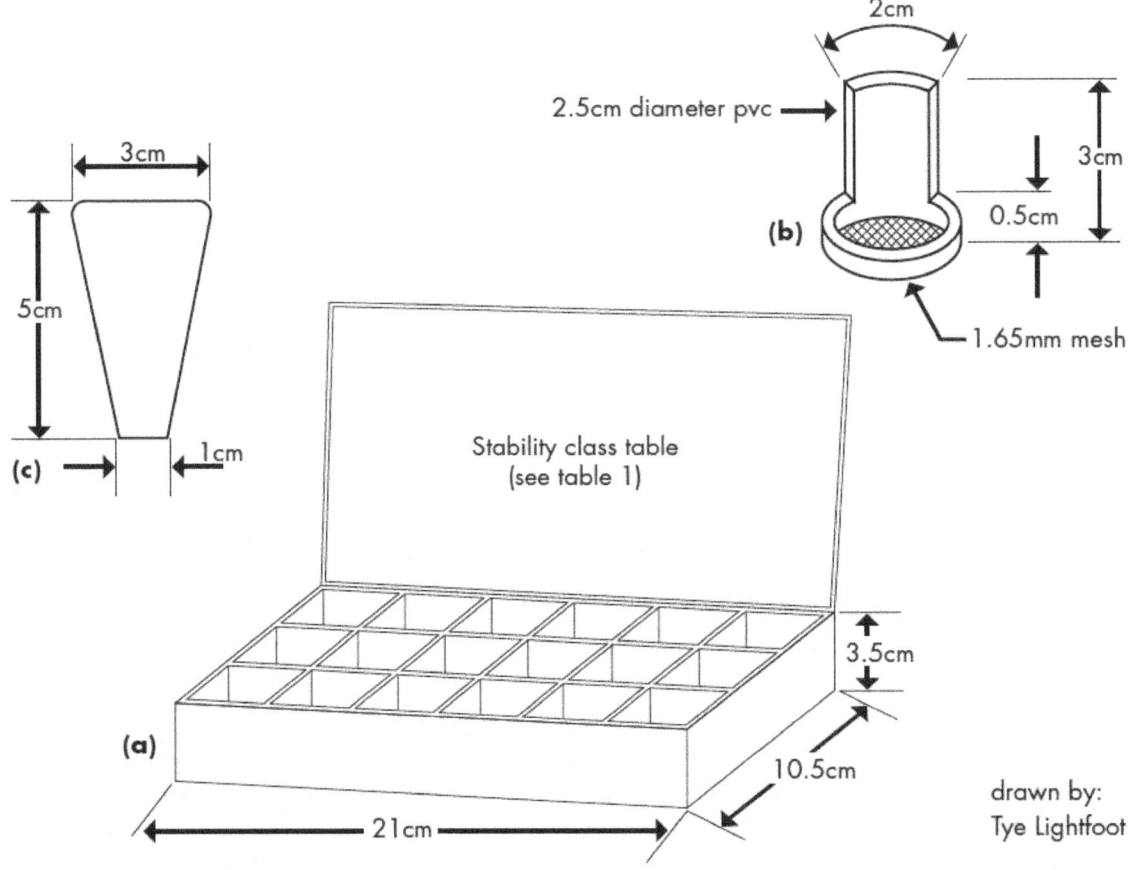

drawn by:
Tye Lightfoot

Adapted from Herrick, J.E., J.W. Van Zee, K.M. Havstad, L.M. Burkett and W.G. Whitford.
2004. Monitoring Manual for Grassland, Shrubland and Savanna Ecosystems.
USDA-ARS Jornada Experimental Range, Las Cruces, NM. Distributed by University of Arizona Press.

Soil Stability Test

Materials

- Complete soil stability kits (available from Synergy Resource Solutions at www.countgrass.com or construct using instructions in Herrick et al. 2001 or Herrick et al. 2005)
- 1 liter (32 oz.) Deionized water (or any noncarbonated bottled water—except mineral water)
- Clipboard, Soil Stability Test Data Form, and pencil
- Stopwatch

Standard Methods (rule set)

With a little practice, it takes about 10 to 15 minutes to sample. It takes about 10 minutes to test 18 samples.

1. Randomly select 18 sampling points and decide whether you will collect surface samples only (1 box), or surface and subsurface samples (2 boxes).
    RULES:
    a. Use 18 randomly selected points along the transects used for line-point and gap intercept measurements.
    b. Record sampling locations (points) under "Pos" on the data form.
    c. Always sample at least 5 cm (2 inches) from any vegetation measurement line.
    d. Include subsurface sample if you are interested in soil erodibility after disturbance.

2. Determine the dominant cover class over the random point and enter into the "Veg" column on the data form.
    RULES:
    a. The area to be classified is as large as the sample area (6 to 8 mm or 1/4 inch in diameter.
    b. Record the dominant cover class in the "Veg" column.
        C = perennial grass, shrub or tree canopy cover
        NC = no perennial grass, shrub or tree canopy cover

3. Collect a surface sample.
    a. Excavate a small trench in front of the area to be sampled (Figure 1).
    b. Lift out a soil fragment and trim it (if necessary) to the correct size.
    c. The soil fragment should be 2 to 3 mm in diameter (the diameter of a wood pencil eraser) (Figures 2 and 3).
    d. Collect samples at the exact point. Move the sample point only if it has been disturbed during previous measurements or the soil surface is protected by a rock or embedded litter. Move the point a standard distance (1 m) and note this change on the data form.
    e. Minimize shattering by:
        - slicing the soil around the sample before lifting;
        - lifting out a larger sample than required, and trimming it to the size of the palm of your hand; or
        - misting the sample area before collection.
    f. If the soil is too weakly structured to sample (falls through the sieve), mist it lightly with deionized water (use an atomizer or equivalent) and then take a sample. Perfume and plastic hair spray bottles work well for this. If the sample still will not hold together, record a "1" on the data form.
    g. If the soil surface is covered by a lichen or cyanobacterial crust, include the crust in the sample. If the sample is covered by moss, collect the sample from under the moss.
    h. Gently place the sample in a dry sieve (Figure 4); place sieve in the appropriate cell of a dry box. Leave the box lid open (Figure 5).

Figure 1. Excavate small trench.

Figure 2. Collect surface sample.

Figure 3. Ensure correct sample size.

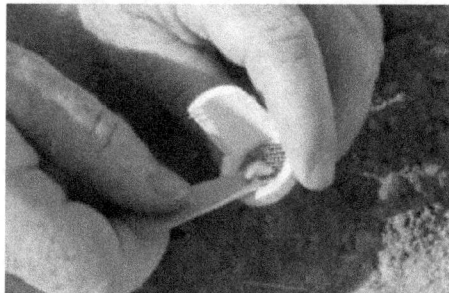

Figure 4. Place sample in sieve.

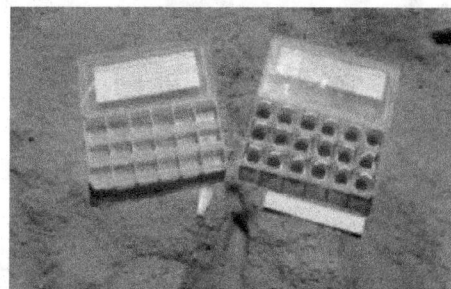

Figure 5. Complete soil stability kit with water and samples.

4. Make sure the surface and subsurface samples are dry.
   a. Samples must be dry before testing. If samples are not dry after collecting, allow to air dry with the lid off.
   b. Do not leave lid closed on samples for more than one minute on hot/sunny days. Excessive heat can artificially increase or decrease stability.

5. Fill the empty (no sieves) box with deionized or distilled water (Figure 5).
   a. Fill each compartment to the top.
   b. The water should be approximately the same temperature as the soil.

6. Test the samples.
   a. Lower the first sieve with the sample into the respective water-filled compartment (the upper left corner of the water box) (Figure 6).
   b. From the time the sieve screen touches the water surface to the time it rests on the bottom of the box, one second should elapse.
   c. Start the stopwatch when the first sample touches the water. Use the table below to assign samples to stability classes.
   d. After five minutes, follow the sequence of immersions on the data form, adding one sample every 15 seconds. Beginners may want to immerse a sample every 30 seconds. This allows nine samples to be run in ten minutes (18 samples in 20 minutes).
   e. Observe the fragments from the time the sample hits the water to five minutes (300 seconds) and record a stability class based on the table below.
   f. Raise the sieve completely out of the water and then lower it to the bottom without touching the bottom of the tray. Repeat this immersion a total of five times. Do this even if you have already rated the sample a 1, 2, or 3. You can change your rating, if after sieving, less than 10 percent of the soil remains on the sieve.
   g. It should take one second for each sieve to clear the water's surface and one second to return to near the bottom of the box.
   h. Hydrophobic samples (samples that float in water after being pushed under) are rated 6.

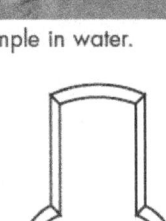

Figure 6. Place first sample in water.

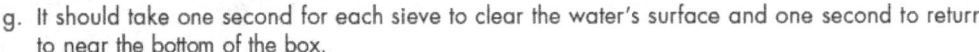

Figure 7. Sample in sieve, drawn to scale.

Bottlecap test (Semiquantitative alternative)
Place a soil fragment in a bottle cap filled with water. Watch it for 30 seconds. Gently swirl the water for five seconds. Assign one of the following three ratings:
   M = Melts in first 30 seconds (without swirling)   **S** = Stable (even after swirling)
   D = Disintegrates when swirls (but does not melt)

Sequence for stability class = 1

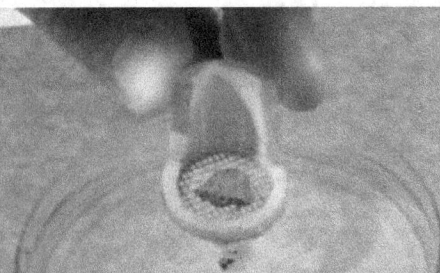

Figure 8A. Original Sample

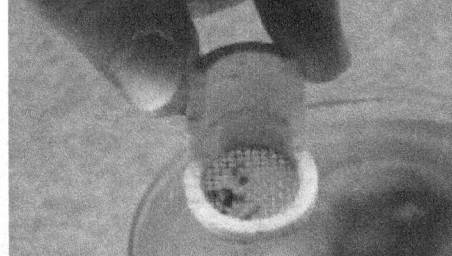

Figure 8B. After 5 Seconds

Figure 8. The photos illustrate the key steps of testing a soil sample for four different stability rankings.

Important Note: Some of the fragments shown in these samples may appear large. They are for illustration only. Be sure to follow the size guidelines.

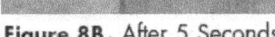

Figure 8C. After 5 Minutes

Figure 8D. After 5 Dips

Sequence for stability class = 4

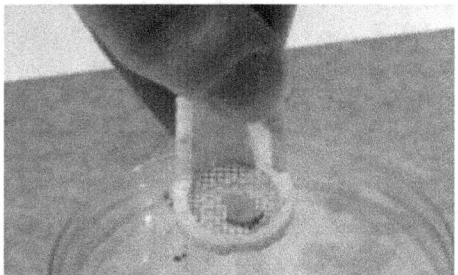

Figure 8E. Original Sample

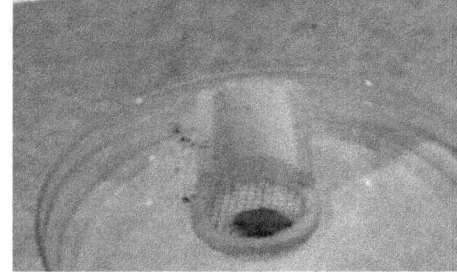

Figure 8F. After 5 Seconds

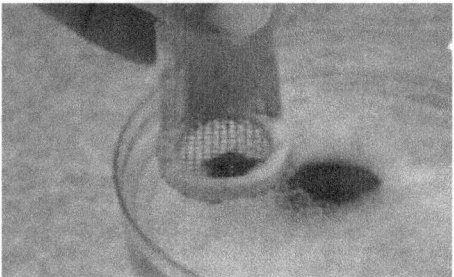

Figure 8G. After 5 Minutes

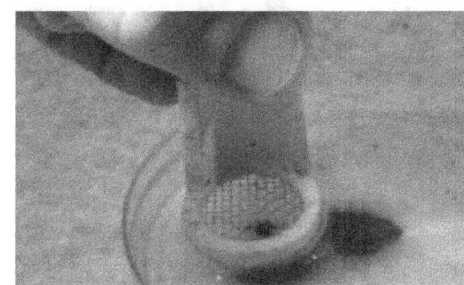

Figure 8H. After 5 Dips

Sequence for stability class = 5

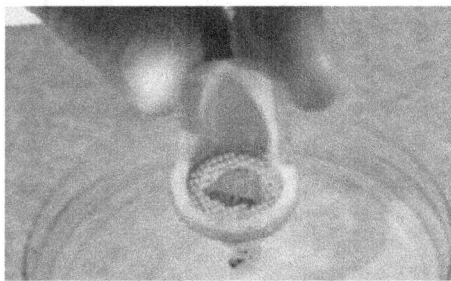

Figure 8I. Original Sample

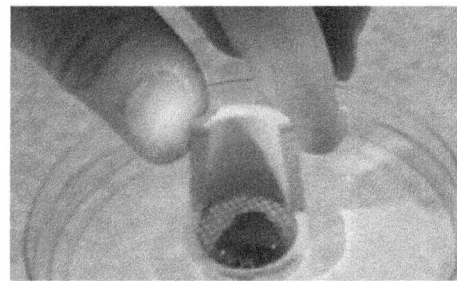

Figure 8J. After 5 Seconds

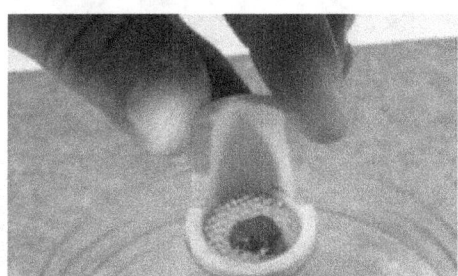

Figure 8K. After 5 Minutes

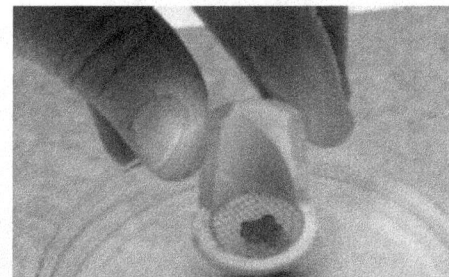

Figure 8L. After 5 Dips

Sequence for stability class = 6

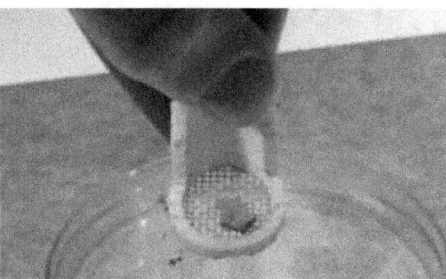

Figure 8M. Original Sample

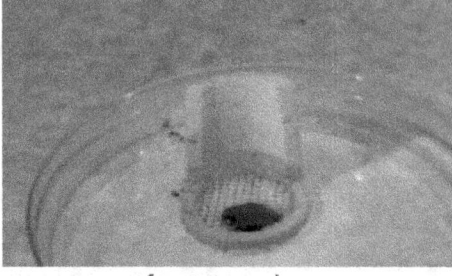

Figure 8N. After 5 Seconds

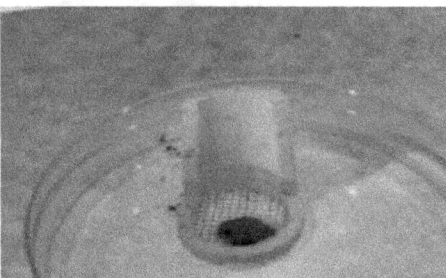

Figure 8O. After 5 Minutes

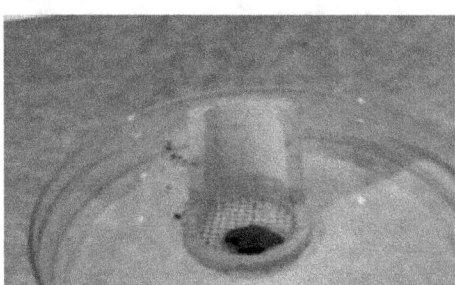

Figure 8P. After 5 Dips

Soil Stability Test Data Form

Monitoring plot: _____ Observer: _____ Date: _____

Recorder: _____ Page ____ of ____

Veg = NC (no perennial canopy), **C** (plant canopy cover). **#** = **Stability value** (1-6). Circle value if samples are hydrophobic. Rate samples beginning in upper left corner and working left to right.

15 Seconds Between Samples

Line	Pos	Veg	In time	Dip time	#
			0:00	5:00	
			1:30	6:30	
			3:00	8:00	

Line	Pos	Veg	In time	Dip time	#
			0:15	5:15	
			1:45	6:45	
			3:15	8:15	

Line	Pos	Veg	In time	Dip time	#
			0:30	5:30	
			2:00	7:00	
			3:30	8:30	

Line	Pos	Veg	In time	Dip time	#
			0:45	5:45	
			2:15	7:15	
			3:45	8:45	

Line	Pos	Veg	In time	Dip time	#
			1:00	6:00	
			2:30	7:30	
			4:00	9:00	

Line	Pos	Veg	In time	Dip time	#
			1:15	6:15	
			2:45	7:45	
			4:15	9:15	

Notes: _____

30 Seconds Between Samples

Line	Pos	Veg	In time	Dip time	#
			0:00	5:00	
			1:00	6:00	

Line	Pos	Veg	In time	Dip time	#
			0:30	5:30	
			1:30	6:30	

Line	Pos	Veg	In time	Dip time	#
			1:00	6:00	
			2:00	7:00	

Line	Pos	Veg	In time	Dip time	#
			1:30	6:30	
			2:30	7:30	

Line	Pos	Veg	In time	Dip time	#
			2:00	7:00	
			3:00	8:00	

Line	Pos	Veg	In time	Dip time	#
			2:30	7:30	
			3:30	8:30	

Line	Pos	Veg	In time	Dip time	#
			3:00	8:00	
			4:00	9:00	

Line	Pos	Veg	In time	Dip time	#
			3:30	8:30	
			4:30	9:30	

Notes: _____

Avg. Stability = Sum of Stability Rankings (i.e., #) / Total No. Samples Taken

Line	All samples Surface	All samples Subsurface	Protected samples (Samples w/Veg = G, Sh, or T) Surface	Protected samples Subsurface	Unprotected samples (Samples w/Veg = NC) Surface	Unprotected samples Subsurface
Plot Avg.						

Appendix 8

Checklist for Rangeland Health Assessment Protocol

Checklist for Rangeland Health Assessment Protocol

Pre-Field Tasks	Who is Responsible	Initial and Date
Individual/team organized or designated		
Soil survey or soil information assembled		
Ecological site description obtained		
Equipment gathered (shovel, soil stability kit, camera, GPS unit, data forms, technical reference, maps, etc.)		
Identify potential reference areas, if desired		
Reference Sheet availability checked and obtain copies for ecological sites in potential evaluation areas		
Step 1. Visit Evaluation Area and Verify Soil and Ecological Site Information		
Soil and ecological site verification		
Complete first page of Evaluation Sheet		
Step 2. Reference Sheet—Obtain or Develop (REQUIRED)		
Obtain reference sheet if available		
If not available STOP until reference sheet is developed		
If reference sheet is draft, undergoes development or revision, send copy to NRCS State Rangeland Management Specialist		
Develop Functional/Structural Groups Sheet (species list and complete the "potential" column		
Visit ecological reference area if available and incorporate information from it in the development of the Reference Sheet.		
Obtain or develop Ecological Site Evaluation Matrix (Information from reference sheet becomes none to slight values in evaluation matrix).		
Step 3. Collect Supplementary Information (OPTIONAL BUT HIGHLY RECOMMENDED)		
Collect quantitative data and spatial and temporal information at the evaluation area. Complete the "Actual" column of the Functional/Structural Sheet		
Step 4. Rate 17 Indicators		
Include written comments to explain/justify all ratings		
Step 5. Evaluate 3 Rangeland Health Attributes		
Include written comments to explain/justify preponderance of evidence ratings for each attribute.